AIR VANGUARD 16

LOCKHEED F-117 NIGHTHAWK STEALTH FIGHTER

PAUL F. CRICKMORE

CIVIC CENTER

First published in Great Britain in 2014 by Osprey Publishing,
PO Box 883, Oxford, OX1 9PL, UK
PO Box 3985, New York, NY 10185-3985, USA
E-mail: info@ospreypublishing.com

Osprey Publishing is part of the Osprey Group

A CIP catalog record for this book is available from the British Library

Print ISBN: 978 1 4728 0116 6
PDF ebook ISBN: 978 1 4728 0117 3
ePub ebook ISBN: 978 1 4728 0118 0

Index by Mark Swift
Typeset in Sabon
Originated by PDQ Media, Bungay, UK
Printed in China through Worldprint Ltd

14 15 16 17 18   10 9 8 7 6 5 4 3 2 1

Osprey Publishing is supporting the Woodland Trust, the UK's leading
woodland conservation charity, by funding the dedication of trees.

www.ospreypublishing.com

AUTHOR'S DEDICATION

To our wonderful granddaughter, Mia.

ACKNOWLEDGEMENTS

Writing a book of this type, I was very reliant upon the generosity of
others, as I was not one of those amazing individuals directly involved
in the F-117's design, development, maintenance or operations. So, to
all that have been so supportive of my efforts, a big thank you; I am
sincerely grateful. There were four individuals, however, that were
exponentially generous with their time and help; to Gabor Zord, Tony
Landis, Yancy Mailes and Lt-Col Brad O'Connor I owe a particular debt
of gratitude. I would also like to thank Flt-Lt Adam Crickmore (RAF),
Kent Burns, Paul Eden, Phil Smith, Tom Milner and Adam Tooby. Last,
but by no means least, all my love and thanks go to Ali, my amazing
wife.

CONTENTS

LOCKHEED F-117 NIGHTHAWK STEALTH FIGHTER

INTRODUCTION

Although universally known as "the Stealth Fighter," Lockheed's F-117 was an attack aircraft. Designed within the legendary Skunk Works primarily by electronic engineers, radically new solutions had to be developed to enable the aircraft to evade radar detection and interception. The enormity of the challenge is neatly conceptualized by the radar equation, which basically states that "radar detection range is proportional to the fourth root of the targets' radar cross section (RCS)." In other words, to reduce the detection range of an aircraft by a factor of ten, it is necessary to reduce its RCS by a factor of 10,000 or 40 dBs. Having successfully vaulted such a monumental hurdle, when the F-117 was deployed in combat, together with its weapons delivery system it achieved a consistent – almost eye-watering – level of success, the like of which had never before been attained by any other previous combat aircraft. Indeed, so deadly accurate was this weapons platform, it enabled US Air Force (USAF) planners to confidently utilize the aircraft against some of the world's most highly defended targets to perform a "surgical strike" – destroying the target without other areas incurring collateral damage.

Perhaps not surprisingly, the F-117 and its forerunners were developed in the "Black World" and flight-tested at the hot, highly classified desert test site known as Area 51. When, finally, the basic shape of the much speculated F-19 stealth fighter was revealed to the public by Assistant Defense Secretary J. Daniel Howard during a Pentagon press conference on November 10, 1988, the grainy photograph depicted a black, stubby, angular aircraft, whose shape was more akin to a lifting body or something that Darth Vader might have flown in a sequence from *Star Wars*. It certainly bore no resemblance whatsoever to the curves and blended body of what was supposedly an accurate representation of the aircraft available for model enthusiasts to purchase in the form of a plastic construction kit. The security clearance necessary to access information relating to the Have Blue proof of concept (or demonstrator) vehicles and the follow-on Senior Trend program (the equally classified code name for the F-117) was categorized as top secret/sensitive compartmented information (TS/SCI), and it was spectacularly successful in keeping both programs under wraps. When Lockheed test pilot Dave Ferguson first saw the highly faceted, unconventional, "slab-sided" aircraft, he asked Dick Cantrell how airframe ice encrustation might affect the aircraft's aerodynamics. The program's chief aerodynamicist dryly replied, "Probably improve it."

When Ben Rich became president of the Skunk Works on January 17, 1975, Lockheed faced financial losses amounting to $2 billion. Selling the U-2R concept to the USAF, together with his strident support of Have Blue and the F-117 program, undoubtedly played a major role in turning around the company's fortunes. (Lockheed Martin)

The less-than-spectacular combat debut of the F-117 during Operation *Just Cause* – the US invasion and subsequent ousting of General Manuel Noriega from Panama – was more than compensated for just 15 months later, on January 17, 1991. On this date, during the opening phase of Operation *Desert Storm* (the expulsion of Saddam Hussein's occupying forces from Kuwait), the first laser-guided bombs dropped from F-117s slammed into their targets with devastating accuracy. Some of the infrared footage of these strikes, recorded in each aircraft for subsequent analysis by pilots and intelligence specialists, was made available to the media, and became a source of fascinating viewing during news bulletins throughout the world. The 43-day campaign proved beyond a shadow of a doubt the effectiveness of stealth technology as applied to the F-117 when, despite flying hundreds of sorties against the most heavily defended targets in Iraq, not a single one of these ungainly looking aircraft was shot down or even hit.

DESIGN AND DEVELOPMENT

Air battles fought by the United States during the Vietnam War, together with losses suffered by Israel during the so-called Yom Kippur War of 1973, were responsible for the Defense Advanced Research Projects Agency (DARPA) initiating conceptual studies into developing a manned aircraft with a sufficiently low RCS to defeat modern air-defense systems. Consequently, in 1974 Ken Perko of the Tactical Technology Office (TTO) at DARPA requested submissions from Northrop, McDonnell Douglas, General Dynamics, Fairchild, and Grumman, under the code name *Project Harvey* (derived from an old movie starring James Stewart and "featuring" an invisible ten-foot rabbit named Harvey), addressing two considerations. Firstly, what were the signature thresholds that an aircraft would need to achieve to become essentially undetectable at an operationally useful range? Secondly, did the relevant companies possess the capabilities to design and produce an aircraft with the necessary low signatures?

Fairchild and Grumman declined the invitation to participate, while General Dynamics emphasized the continued need for electronic countermeasures. However, the submissions from McDonnell Douglas and Northrop demonstrated both a grasp of the problem and a degree of technical capability for developing an aircraft with a reduced signature. Consequently, both companies were awarded contracts worth approximately $100,000 each during the closing months of 1974 to conduct further studies. Radar experts from the Hughes Aircraft Company were also involved, their role being to identify and verify appropriate RCS thresholds. At this early stage the studies were only classified as "Confidential."

Bill Elsner was the primary USAF technical expert on the program, and by the beginning of 1975 McDonnell Douglas had identified likely RCS thresholds that could produce an operational advantage. In the spring, these were confirmed by Hughes and were established by DARPA as goals for the program. DARPA then challenged the participants to find ways of achieving them.

Lockheed had not been one of the five original companies approached by DARPA, simply because it had not produced a fighter for nearly ten years. This, however, was about to change. Whilst networking his contacts at the Pentagon and Wright-Patterson Air Force Base (AFB), Ed Martin, Lockheed California Company's Director for Science and Engineering, was made aware of the study. He flagged this to Ben Rich, who at this time was deputy to the Skunk Works' legendary president Clarence L. "Kelly" Johnson. The two men then briefed Johnson, who in turn obtained a letter from the Central Intelligence Agency (CIA), granting the Skunk Works permission to discuss with DARPA the low observable (LO) characteristics of their earlier A-12 and D-21 drone program.

Rich and Martin presented this data to Ken Perko and Doctor George Heilmeier, the head of DARPA, and formally requested entry into the competition. However, Heilmeier explained that two $100,000 contracts had already been awarded and there was no more cash available. Drawing upon his negotiation skills, Rich convinced the DARPA boss to allow Lockheed into the competition without a government contract – a move that ultimately paid a handsome dividend. The Skunk Works team were then given access to technical reports already provided to the other participants, and the first step that would culminate in a revolutionary aircraft was taken.

Within the Skunk Works team, Denys Overholser recalls his boss, Dick Scherrer, asking him one day, "How do we shape something to make it invisible to radar?" Overholser's reply was, "Well, it's simple, you just make

F-117 PROFILES

1: The Have Blue prototype HB1001 (known in-house as Blue 1) had a unique camouflage pattern applied at Burbank before being disassembled and flown via C-5 Galaxy to the test site at Area 51.

2: The second Have Blue aircraft, HB1002, first flew on July 20, 1978. It was flown primarily to enable various air- and ground-based radars to gather RCS data. It completed 52 sorties before crashing on July 11, 1979.

3: The F-117 prototype aircraft 780 sported an unusual camouflage pattern for its first ten test flights, before being painted light gray for over a year.

4: When aircraft 781 completed its flight-test career, it was bead-blasted of all its classified, radar-absorbent coatings, and generally stripped out inside, before undergoing a functional check flight (as depicted here). It was then delivered to the US Air Force Museum, where it received a coat of standard black paint before being put on display.

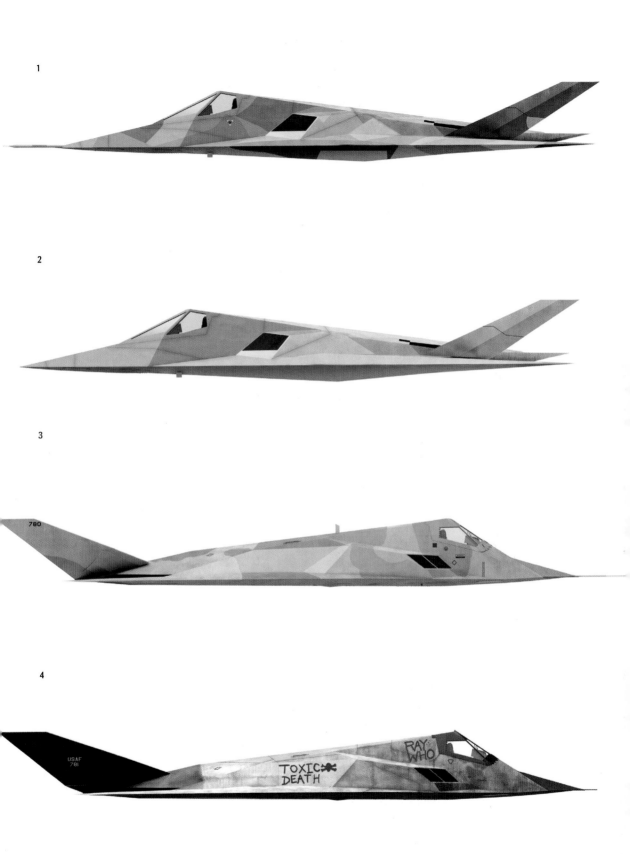

it out of flat surfaces, and you tilt those flat surfaces over, sweeping the edges away from the radar view angle, and that way you basically cause the energy to reflect away from the radar, thus limiting the magnitude of the return." The framework for such radical thinking had its roots in discussions that Overholser had had years earlier with his then-boss Bill Schroeder. Schroeder, a brilliant mathematician, had been employed by Johnson to resolve analytical problems, and had trained Overholser. During the course of discussing the mathematics and physics of optical scattering, the two had concluded that detectable signatures could be minimized by utilizing a shape composed of the smallest number of properly orientated flat panels. In addition, Schroeder believed that he could develop and resolve a mathematical equation capable of calculating analytically the reflection from a triangular flat panel; this in turn could be applied in a calculation relating to RCS.

With input from Overholser, Scherrer drew a preliminary low-RCS shape based upon a faceted delta wing. By April, Bill Schroeder had been brought into the team and set about completing solutions to RCS equations that would enable the group eventually to predict results. Kenneth Watson was appointed Senior Lead Aircraft Designer, tasked with positioning all systems inside the "shell" that Scherrer and Overholser were designing.

As Schroeder's mathematical computations became available, Overholser and his team of two engineers then used these to write the computer program that could evaluate the RCS of prospective design submissions nominated by Dick Scherrer. Overholser and his team worked night and day, and in just five weeks produced an RCS prediction program known as Echo 1. However, as tests continued, it became apparent that the edge contributions calculated by Echo 1 were not accurate, due to a phenomenon known as diffraction.

Incredibly, a solution to this problem was provided by a Soviet scientist. The Skunk Works team were made aware of an article entitled "Method of Edge Waves in the Physical Theory of Diffraction," published in an unclassified technical paper by Pyotr Ufimtsev (Chief Scientist at the Moscow Institute of Radio Engineering), which had been translated by Air Force Systems Command's Foreign Technology Division in 1971. Overholser was able to incorporate elements of its theory into a refined version of the Echo 1 program and use this to mathematically evaluate over 20 designs to identify the one with the smallest RCS. The faceted delta wing design had more than its share of sceptics within the Skunk Works. Some in aerodynamics referred to the shape as "the Hopeless Diamond."

Two one-third-scale wooden models of the Hopeless Diamond were constructed. One was used by the aerodynamists in wind tunnel tests, and the other was coated with metal foil to provide a conductive surface and used to measure RCS values in Lockheed's anechoic chamber. The first series of tests were conducted in June 1975, and they demonstrated that the RCS "spikes" matched precisely those predicted by Echo 1. The model was then moved outdoors to the Gray Butte Radar Test Range which boasted improved capabilities and enabled the team to measure even lower RCS values. Yet again, these test results conformed well to Echo 1 predictions, creating greater levels of confidence in both the computer program and the faceted design concept.

The Northrop full-scale model demonstrator undertaking RCS tests during Phase 1 of the Experimental Survivable Testbed (XST) program at the USAF RATSCAT facility at White Sands, New Mexico in February 1976. (Northrop via Tony Landis)

To improve the vehicle's lift-to-drag ratio, the section outboard the engine inlets was thinned, resulting in the semblance of wings. These were eventually extended outward, changing the planform from the original diamond shape to a notched-out delta. The trailing edge sweep was increased to 48 degrees to ensure that the signature spike, associated with the trailing edge, fell outside the frontal sector. To minimize "nose-on" detection, inboard canted tail surfaces were also added.

Two proposals were submitted to DARPA from Lockheed. One included the predicted and measured signature data for the Hopeless Diamond; the other provided the predicted data for an air vehicle of flyable configuration. This came about in response to DARPA issuing proposals to the three competitors for what was to become known as the Experimental Survivable Testbed (XST) program. This was informally requested in the late summer of 1975 and responses were due in August or September; the signature goals therein were those laid down in the earlier 1974/1975 directive.

Northrop's XST entry was similar in appearance to that of Lockheed's. Its design had been developed from a computer program called GENSCAT, which also had its origins in mathematical equations associated with the physics of optics. Like Lockheed, Northrop used both computer modeling and the Gray Butte Range (near Palmdale, California) to test and evaluate their design. By the summer of 1975 they, too, had reliable indications that their design would achieve the RCS goals set earlier.

Having been the first to determine what the RCS thresholds for the competition were likely to be, McDonnell Douglas were unable to design an aircraft that could achieve anything like those goals. With RCS results coming from both Lockheed and Northrop verging on the revolutionary, Ken Perko called a meeting within DARPA to determine the program's future direction. It was decided that the program should be developed still further, into a full-scale, flight-test demonstration, consisting of two phases. Phase 1 would culminate in a ground RCS evaluation of large-scale models. Following this, one contractor would be selected to proceed with Phase 2, the construction and flight-testing of two demonstration vehicles. The estimated cost for the XST program was $36 million and this would be borne by and split between the successful contractor, a reluctant USAF, and DARPA. The latter would contribute marginally more, thereby retaining program management control. By August 1975 funding arrangements were completed and on November 1, Lockheed and Northrop were awarded contracts of $1.5 million each to conduct Phase 1 of the XST program.

The two companies were each given just four months to complete the initial phase of the competition, which involved the construction of full-scale, wooden test models. These would then be evaluated at the Air Force's radar target scatter (RATSCAT) test range, located at White Sands, New Mexico. It was already apparent that the RCS results achieved by both participating companies were unlike anything obtained before, and it became necessary to develop a new, lower-signature pylon so that returns from the pylon did not impinge upon results from the test models.

The Lockheed model was hauled by truck to RATSCAT for testing in March. Throughout the tests the competing contractors and their models were kept in isolation from one another, billeted in temporary quarters affording each independent access to the range. In early April 1976 Lockheed received word that they had officially won Phase 1 of the competition.

However, the outstanding results achieved by Northrop caused DARPA to urge its team to remain together. Shortly thereafter, DARPA initiated studies into a Battlefield Surveillance Aircraft, Experimental (BSAX), which eventuated into Tacit Blue – the highly successful flight demonstration program that provided vital data for the subsequent B-2 bomber program.

Lockheed undertook RCS testing of their small-scale Have Blue models in their anechoic chamber located at Rye Canyon. (Lockheed Martin)

HAVE BLUE

Since US Air Force Systems Command (AFSC) sponsored Phase 2 of the XST program, protocol dictated that the code name was prefixed "Have." It was therefore accorded the name Have Blue and was initiated on April 26, 1976. The Skunk Works were authorized to proceed with their winning design for the construction and flight-testing of two technology demonstrator aircraft. Ben Rich secured $10.4 million from Lockheed Corporation and contract negotiations were completed two months later. The first flight was scheduled for December 1977.

Have Blue had three objectives:

1. Validate in flight the four low observability signatures identified earlier in the program (radar, infrared, acoustic, and visual);
2. Demonstrate acceptable performance and flying qualities;
3. Demonstrate modeling capabilities that accurately predict low observable characteristics of an aircraft in flight.

Manufacturing of Have Blue was placed under the direction of Bob Murphy, and the entire engineering, fabrication and assembly of the two aircraft was carried out in Building 82 (birthplace of the F-104, U-2, and A-12). Just four assembly tools were used on the project, comprising wing, forward fuselage, aft fuselage, boom, and stub fin assembly sections.

By early 1977 the government realized that a major breakthrough had been achieved in very low observable (VLO) technology and that its impact on national defense would be profound. Consequently, program security catapulted from the White World minimum security classification of Confidential, into the Black World categorization of TS/SCI.

General Alton Slay, Deputy Chief of Staff for USAF Research and Development, appointed Lt-Col Larry McClain as flight-test director at Area 51. Major Jack Twigg became the System Program Officer (SPO), whose remit was to procure, wherever possible, tried and tested, off-the-shelf pieces of equipment to save money. These would then be delivered into Building 82, via circuitous, covert routes, in order to retain tight security.

The two Have Blue aircraft (referred to by Lockheed as Blue 01 and Blue 02), were single-seat, subsonic machines, each powered by two 2,950lb (13.12kN) thrust, General Electric J85-GE-4A non-afterburning engines. Six engines were acquired for the program from the US Navy's North American T-2B Buckeye trainer stores.

Have Blue was 47.25ft long, 7.54ft high and had a span of 22.5ft. Its modified delta wing planform had a sweep of 72.5 degrees, creating a wing area of 386 square feet. No flaps, speed brakes, or high-lift devices were incorporated into the structure, which was built mainly from aluminum alloy, utilizing steel and titanium in the hot areas. Aerodynamic control was achieved by ailerons, located inboard on the wings, and by two all-movable fins that were canted inboard about 30 degrees. Flight control actuators were the same as those used on the F-111. A small side-stick controller (YF-16 stock) and conventional rudder pedals enabled the pilot to operate the control surfaces. The external shape evolved from VLO and controllability considerations, the fallout from which was a relaxed static stability (RSS) aircraft, which required a quad-redundant fly-by-wire (FBW) flight control system to provide handling qualities throughout the flight envelope. The FBW system that provided stability augmentation was made by Lear-Seigler (also F-16 stock) – there was no mechanical back-up.

During the course of aerodynamic tests conducted by the Skunk Works on free-flight models, it was determined that the large leading-edge wing sweep produced considerable nose-up pitch moments, actually causing pitch departure when 17 degrees angle-of-attack (AOA) was exceeded.

HB1001 had this unique camouflage pattern applied by Alan Brown (Chief Technical Engineer) and Ben Dehaven whilst it was still at Burbank. Consisting of three different colors with each color having three different tones, it was applied in such a way as to hide the faceting from any casual uncleared "onlookers." The aircraft is seen here on the ramp at Area 51. (Lockheed Martin)

To prevent such events occurring on the two Have Blue aircraft, elevon "nose-down" pitch control was augmented by a large, two-position flap which comprised the trailing edge of the exhaust deck. Called the "platypus," it automatically deflected downward whenever 13 degrees AOA was exceeded. The platypus flap then retracted automatically after the pilot reduced the aircraft's angle-of-attack.

Externally, the two Have Blue aircraft differed slightly from one another. The prototype HB1001 was equipped with a large flight-test nose boom and a chute for spin recovery, which was unstealthily mounted in an external box on top of the fuselage. Since this aircraft would only be used to validate handling qualities, the non-stealthy nature of this arrangement was not an issue. HB1002, however, was designated as the RCS test vehicle. Gross weight of the aircraft ranged from 9,200 to 12,500lb; zero fuel weight was 8,950lb with 3,500lb of fuel being carried in fuselage and wing tanks. VLO requirements resulted in the design of a unique exhaust system. To prevent radar energy from penetrating to and reflecting back from the turbine face, the tailpipe was transitioned from a round duct to a 17-to-1 flattened, slot convergent nozzle. In addition, bypass air was passed over the tailpipe to cool the aft fuselage structure, thereby reducing the infrared (IR) signature. Major Norman "Ken" Dyson was selected as the AF pilot on the project, and he worked closely with Bill Park, Lockheed's Chief Test Pilot on Have Blue.

During HB1001's third high-speed taxi test the brakes overheated, causing the wheel fuse plugs to melt. This became an ongoing problem for the aircraft, with its high approach and touchdown speed. Bill Park is pictured with his nautical answer to the problem. (Lockheed Martin via Tony Landis)

On November 16, 1977, the disassembled and crated Have Blue prototype was flown out from Burbank to Area 51 in the belly of a C-5A Galaxy. At the test site the aircraft was reassembled, and after completing four low- and high-speed taxi tests, the aircraft was cleared to fly at 0700 hours on December 1. Park flew Blue-01 on its maiden flight, and despite a strong headwind, the takeoff run was long and climb-out sluggish, due to the aircraft's low lift-to-drag and its low thrust-to-weight ratios. Additional power loss was also associated with the inlet grids and the engine exhausts. The gear remained extended to avoid retraction problems and the flight was completed satisfactorily.

By May 4, 1978, Park had successfully completed 24 flights on HB1001 and Dyson had notched up 12. Although the aircraft had performed well throughout the flight-test program, things went wrong on that day. As Park crossed the runway threshold at about 113kts, descending at about 1ft per second, the platypus extended to reduce the AOA. Just three or four feet above the runway, the aircraft pitched downwards. Park managed to get the nose up, but the aircraft impacted the runway hard, starboard main gear first. With both mains on the deck, the flight control system logic worked as designed and rapidly retracted the platypus. This, however, caused the aircraft to pitch into a high AOA. Park regained control, increased power, called that he was "Going around," and instinctively retracted the undercarriage. Unfortunately, the starboard gear leg had been bent during runway impact and refused to extend from the wheel well during subsequent landing approaches. Park was therefore instructed to climb to 10,000ft and eject. However, during the climb the engines flamed out due to lack of fuel, and Park ejected earlier than planned. Unfortunately, he was injured whilst exiting the aircraft and was unconscious when he hit the desert floor. He was quickly recovered by a paramedic and taken to hospital where he later made a full recovery. Having received concussion, Park's flight-test career was unfortunately brought to a close.

HB1002 was flown throughput its test career by Lt-Col Ken Dyson, and was the nominated RCS test vehicle. (Lockheed Martin)

Blue-02 undertook its first flight with Dyson at the controls on July 20, 1978. Three further flights were made, during which the flight control systems, hydraulics, engine, and the data collecting system were fully checked. On August 9, 1978, the first airborne RCS measurements were taken. By June 29, 1979, Dyson had flown HB1002 against every operational radar system they had access to, with measurements having been taken from every possible angle. On July 11 Dyson flew against an F-15 Eagle to monitor how its radar performed against the strange-looking craft. Just short of a designated turn point, Dyson noticed that one of the hydraulic systems begin to oscillate in the downward direction, so he decided to abort the sortie and head back to home plate (Area 51). He was in the process of informing test control about the problem when he got a fire-warning light. Pulling the power back, he shut the engine down. Things seemed to settle down, with the aircraft heading in the right direction between 20,000 and 25,000ft and configured at the right speed for single-engine operation, when hydraulic power in the remaining system began to drop. Dyson then lost hydraulic pressure on the remaining system. The aircraft pitched down suddenly and violently, approximately seven negative-g. According to Dyson, "It then pitched up at an eye-watering rate, something only an unstable machine could do." The aircraft was traveling at around 225kts and above 20,000ft and tossing up and down, with near-vertical nose-down one moment and near-vertical nose-up the next. Dyson ejected, and from under the chute he watched as the aircraft impacted the ground and erupted into a ball of fire.

The cause of the crash was eventually determined to have been the failure of a fuel pipe, which had triggered a fire in the engine compartment. It appears that the hydraulic leak was a separate issue, secondary to the fire. Fortunately, the program was within two or three sorties of its planned completion, which officially ended in December 1979. Having achieved all its test objectives, the Have Blue program was a stunning success. The next challenge was to determine how the demonstrated technology could be integrated into an operational weapons platform.

Despite losing out to Lockheed during Phase 1 of the XST program, DARPA urged the Northrop team to remain together and shortly afterwards initiated studies for a Battlefield Surveillance Aircraft, Experimental (BSAX). This eventuated into the Tacit Blue program – a highly successful flight demonstration program that provided vital data for the subsequent B-2 bomber program. Also known as the YF-117D, Tacit Blue's unusual appearance earned it the nickname "Whale." (Northrop via Tony Landis)

SENIOR TREND

By June 1977 DARPA fully grasped the extent and implications of stealth breakthroughs coming from the XST program, and moved to capitalize on the technology. In turn, the USAF briefed five handpicked officers about the Have Blue program and hid them in the Strategic Reconnaissance Office (AF/RDJP, Room 5D156) in the Pentagon. Reporting directly to General Slay, they became known as the "Gang of Five" and consisted of Col Dave Williams and Majors Ken Staten, Joe Ralston, Bob Swarts, and Jerry Baber. Their remit was to exploit the VLO technology then being demonstrated in Phase 1 of the XST program, and establish a new set of capabilities for the Air Force as quickly as possible and in absolute secrecy.

In addition to initiating conceptual studies into a manned strike-aircraft program, referred to as the Advanced Technology Aircraft (ATA) program, the team also identified the need to develop, in parallel with the XST program, methods of locating, tracking, and striking targets in a way commensurate with maintaining a VLO profile. In response to a request for further information from General Slay, a nine-point document was provided to the SPO, from the vice commander of AFSC, which outlined various stealth-driven programs that would comply with such criteria. One particular line item referred to the development of a forward-looking infrared (FLIR) turret.

Two sets of preliminary requirements for the ATA were developed: ATA "A," a single-seat attack aircraft with a 5,000lb payload and 400nmi range; and ATA "B," a two-seat bomber with a 10,000lb payload and 1,000nmi range. An $11.1 million concept-definition contract was awarded to the Skunk Works on October 10, 1977, for a one-year study, based on the two sets of requirements. The engine selection process began on January 17, 1978, and 11 days later a wind tunnel program was inaugurated, with test results from the Ames Research Center being made available on August 16 that same year.

To achieve the required range, whilst remaining within other stated parameters, it became necessary to reduce the proposed payload of ATA "B" to 7,500lb. As the assimilation continued, it became increasing apparent that ATA "B" was probably beyond what was at that time realistically achievable. Consequently, in the summer of 1978, USAF officials terminated further studies involving ATA "B" and instead opted to move ATA "A" into full-scale development (FSD) – a hitherto unprecedented move.

B

F-117 PROFILES

1: Under program "Evening Shade," aircraft 782 undertook 14 flights from July 12 to October 7, 1993, painted gray. During this series of ground visibility tests, its pilots used the callsign "Gray Ghost."

2: Another unusual evaluation of LO technology was undertaken during mid-1993. During Senior Spud, aircraft 784 had the left side of the fuselage and the inside of the twin fins covered with a textured metallic surface that reflected light in a unique way. The light gray stripe, applied to the aircraft's otherwise black right wing, was an early gray paint under development for the F-22 Raptor. Only four flights were made with this material applied.

3: Aircraft 837, depicted as when at Tonopah Test Range. The Air Combat Command logo is on the tail. The 37th FW's emblem is on both sides of the fuselage and the name "Capt Matt Byrd" (in white) is on the cockpit rail.

4: Aircraft 816, depicted as when at Holloman AFB, New Mexico. Designated the 7th FS commander's aircraft, the 49th FW patch was applied to the right side of fuselage and the 7th FS patch on the left fuselage. The twin tails carry the squadron's motto, "Screamin' Demons."

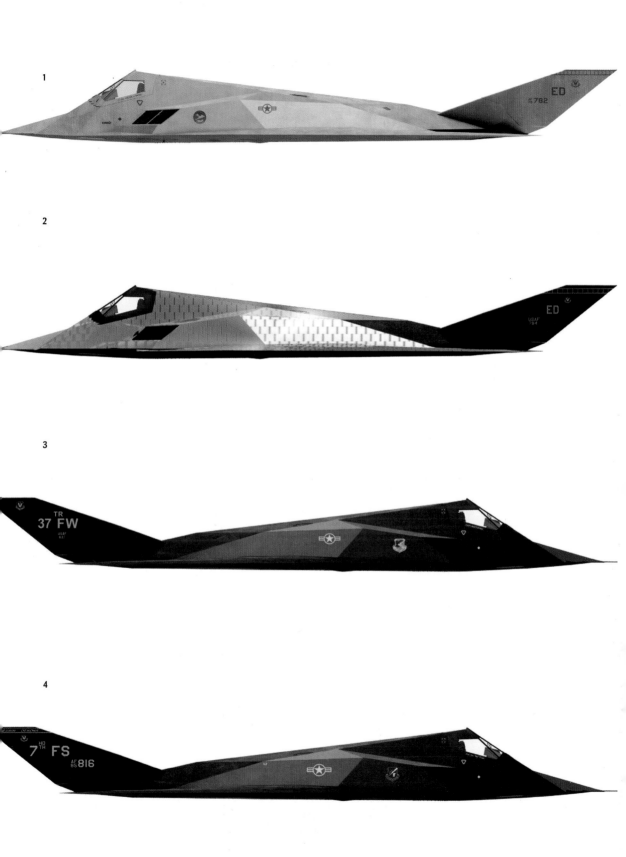

1

2

3

4

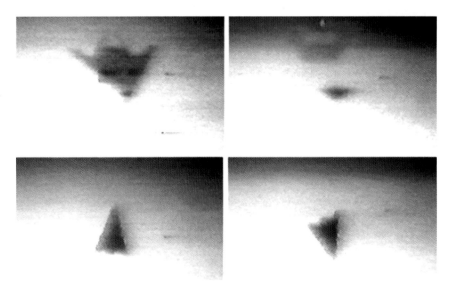

This sequence of four images depicts the demise of HB1001 on May 4, 1978. They are frame-grabs from Area 51's long-range tracking video, and show the aircraft in level flight with the gear down; Bill Park's ejection; and the vehicle completely departing the flight envelope and tumbling out of control to the ground. (Lockheed Martin via Tony Landis)

Covert funds were established, and key individuals serving on the House Appropriations Committee (HAC), the House Armed Services Committee (HASC), the Senate Appropriations Committee (SAC), and the Senate Armed Services Committee (SASC) were briefed on the program. On November 1, 1978, production was authorized, and the program was accorded the classified code name Senior Trend. On November 16, 1978, Lockheed were awarded a full-scale engineering development (FSED) contract for 20 operational aircraft, plus five FSD airframes. The covert squadron operating the ATA would utilize the new platform to "negate anticipated (1990) Soviet defenses." As stated in the Senior Trend acquisition plan, "The principal targets would be command and control communications centers, air defense facilities, airfields, and logistic chokepoints, and other targets of high military interest."

Development of Senior Trend and other LO programs was transferred from the SPO (under Col Dave Williams at the Pentagon) to a newly established SPO under Air Force Systems Command's Aeronautical Systems Division (ASD), located at Wright-Patterson AFB, Ohio. It was known initially as the Classified Aeronautical Systems Program Office (later redesignated the Directorate of Low Observables). Its first director was Col David B. Englund, and Col Eldred D. (Don) Merkl become the Air Force's first Senior Trend Program Manager. Contracting Officer Lt-Col Jerry Baber transferred over from the Pentagon into the Senior Trend SPO.

Production timescales for this revolutionary aircraft program were tight – its first flight was planned for July 1980, hence the last three digits of the prototype's serial number 780 (allocation of this serial number in the Black World was to have repercussions when the aircraft was later integrated into the wider Air Force, as several sequential serials were replicated by other aircraft developed in the White World). Initial Operational Capability (IOC) for the aircraft was to be achieved in March 1982.

On January 1, 1979, construction of a full-scale, wooden mock-up began. Eleven months later, on December 3, the assembly was completed, and functional engineers then used this representation to determine where to situate various aircraft subsystems (such activities have now been superseded by advances in computer software). Construction of FSD-1 – the prototype F-117A (serial 780) – commenced at Burbank in November 1979.

FLIGHT-TESTING

Following recovery from his near-fatal accident in the Have Blue prototype, Lockheed's chief pilot Bill Park began recruiting the initial cadre of company test pilots into the Senior Trend program. The first to be poached was Hal Farley from Grumman, next came Dave Ferguson (then on his final USAF tour as commander of the 6513th Test Squadron, "Red Hats" – the unit flying covertly acquired MiGs up at Area 51), and then came ex-USN pilot Tom Morgenfeld (who had flown MiGs concurrently with both the 6513th and the 4477th Test Evaluation Squadron "Red Eagles" at Tonopah Test Range, the soon-to-be operational home of Senior Trend).

In addition to contractor (Lockheed) pilots, it had been decided that developmental testing, together with category I and II operational test and evaluation (OT&E) of the F-117A would be conducted by a joint test force. Tactical Air Command (TAC) controlled testing, and initially provided three pilots and two analysts. These numbers grew as preparations for the first operational squadron got underway. The third party involved in this "tripartite" force was AFSC, which provided three pilots, four engineers, and approximately 40 aircraft maintenance personnel. Known as the Joint Test Force (JTF) and later renamed the Combined Test Force (CTF), in keeping with the Have Blue program the unit would also be based at Area 51 and was designated Detachment 5 (Det 5). It was headed up by Lt-Col Skip Anderson, who reported in parallel to both Col Pete Winters, commander of the Air Force Flight Test Center (AFFTC) at Edwards AFB and Col Don Merkl, program manager at the SPO.

To prepare themselves for the first series of flights in the F-117, Anderson recalls, "We spent a lot of time with Bob Loschke in the Lockheed simulator out at Rye Canyon, working the control problems. We also flew F-16s on a few occasions because it too was a fly-by-wire system, plus we practiced the F-117's early flight profiles in F-4s and T-38s." In addition, they flew the Calspan NT-33, varying the stability in pitch and yaw, performing takeoffs and landings and degrading the flight characteristics below the air data they had, in order to see if they could land it. Farley recalls, "It turned out to be a valuable learning process for us; the airplane was flyable in its degraded state and this gave us some confidence that even if the air data was wrong, we would be able to get it [the F-117] back on the ground safely."

Upon delivery from Burbank via C-5 Galaxy to Area 51 on January 17, 1981, the prototype F-117 (Aircraft 780) underwent reassembly and a detailed checkout of all onboard systems. It made its first flight five months later. (Lockheed Martin)

Aircraft 780 sported a unique camouflage paint scheme during the first ten flights of its test program. Note the large test instrumentation nose boom. (Lockheed Martin)

Back at Burbank, the Skunk Works ran into many construction problems associated not just with developing a revolutionary airframe, but also with the integration of advanced avionics systems that were either in their infancy or not yet even fielded. Perhaps not surprisingly, the planned first flight date consistently slipped throughout 1980 and into early 1981. However, on January 16, 1981, a C-5 from Burbank touched down at Groom Lake; onboard was Aircraft 780, FSD-1 – the JTF at last had an aircraft.

At 0605 hours on June 18, 1981, "Bandit 01" (Hal Farley later changed his Bandit callsign to Bandit 117, as, unbeknown to him at the time, Bandit numbers 1 through 100 were reserved for the clandestine "Red Hat" and "Red Eagle" MiG pilots) began his takeoff roll, getting airborne a few knots earlier than target speed. The flight went well until a temperature buildup in the exhaust section caused Dick Burton, who was on the ground monitoring the aircraft's systems, to call for an abort. So, aircraft 780 was returned to roost about 15 minutes after takeoff – the undercarriage remaining down throughout the flight.

Farley took to the air in 780 again on July 1 for a flight that lasted 35 minutes, and evaluated the low end of the aircraft's flying characteristics. During this flight Farley retracted the gear and instantly the aircraft yawed. Realizing there was a stability issue, he landed, and after some debate the engineers agreed that the tail fins did not have enough authority and therefore needed to be larger. By this time three of the other FSD aircraft had already had the smaller fins mounted, and this potentially had all the hallmarks of seriously delaying the entire test program.

Flight-testing continued, however. The first six flights were flown by Farley, after which Col Skip Anderson flew 780, thereby becoming the first USAF pilot to fly the ATA. After completion of the tenth flight the prototype was laid up for four months, during which time various modifications were made, including installation of a partial heat shield. The engineers had also devised a fix for the yaw issue by adding fillets to the leading and trailing edges of the existing fins, thereby increasing their overall area by 100 percent, yet still retaining the original RCS spec. Aircraft 781 and 782 both had their stabs replaced at Area 51, whilst the rest of the fleet had modified fins fitted as they came down the assembly line.

Having had its earlier camouflage scheme removed, 780 returned to work sporting an overall gray paint scheme in late October 1981. The aircraft was air-refuel qualified by Skip Anderson on November 17 that year – an action that accelerated the test program by increasing flight duration time. As flight-testing started to ratchet up, on November 27, 1981, the SPO, cognizant of the earlier delays, set a new IOC date for mid-June 1982. The planned target goals for IOC were to have available ten deployable combat aircraft, ten fully trained operational pilots, three full-scale weapons for delivery (Mk-84, GBU-10, SUU-30, and the goal of a B-61), two training weapons (BDU-33 and Mk-106), a 6g load limit, and ability for level delivery. However, as Lockheed battled with issues surrounding icing on the grids covering the engine's air intakes, pitot tube heating that still did not work, and how to cover the cavities within which the FLIR/DLIR (downward-looking infrared radar) was located in a way that radar could not see in but its laser could see out, it became apparent that IOC would need to slip again – this time to October 1983.

As flight-handling and envelope expansion tests continued on the prototype, FSD-2 (serial 781) carried out a series of initial airborne RCS tests. This involved the application of sheets of BX210 RAM (radar-absorbent material), and the flight tests, conducted by Maj Roger Moseley, proved extremely encouraging. On June 11, 1986, aircraft 818 became the first F-117 to have a radar-absorbent coat of BX199 applied robotically. Four years later another program was initiated to further improve the material's durability and maintainability, and by mid-1993 a substance designated BX185 had been successfully developed. Work then began on upgrading the rest of the fleet.

FSD-3 (serial 782) was the dedicated avionics testbed, whilst serial 783 was earmarked for exhaustive low observability testing. The first test of the latter began against an NKC-135 on July 15, 1982, to ascertain the aircraft's IR signature. These tests continued against an F-4 Phantom II, before broadening out to include RCS testing both cued and uncued, against ground and airborne threats.

During 780's first period of downtime from August 6, 1981, to October 21, 1981, the aircraft was repainted in an overall, low-visibility gray scheme. The operational fleet was painted black, despite Lockheed's Alan Brown being able to prove scientifically that gray was the best LO scheme for the aircraft. (Lockheed Martin)

Eleven of the first 13 pilots to fly the F-117 are pictured in front of Aircraft 782. They are, from left to right: Hal Farley, Skip Anderson, Dave Ferguson, Tom Morganfeld, Roger Moseley, Tom Abel, Jon Beesley, Paul Tackabury, Pete Barnes, Denny Mangum, and Dale Irving. Missing are Skip Holm and Bob Riedenauer. (Lockheed Martin via Tony Landis)

Paul Tackabury notched up another milestone in the aircraft's development on December 17, 1982, when during the course of a 1.4-hour test sortie in aircraft 782 he successfully completed the first weapons release from an F-117, dropping an Mk-106 practice bomb from its BDU-33 canister while in level flight.

Aircraft 783 continued to be the fleet's RCS workhorse throughout 1984, with analysis of the air-to-air threat continuing. On April 24 that year, an F-16 made four radar passes against the aircraft while it was being piloted by Morgenfeld. Two days later the same aircraft saw an F-16 make 13 passes against it, and by July 23 F-15s, F-14s, and an EF-111 had conducted similar threat tests. Thereafter, 783 was used alternately between low-observability tests and the integration and evaluation of improvements made to the navigation and weapons delivery systems.

FSD-5, aircraft 784, was the dedicated infrared acquisition designation system (IRADS) testbed, and its first 106 flights were conducted in association with achieving the successful integration and operation of this unique weapons delivery system. It was placed in temporary storage on completion of a sortie flown by Roger Moseley on September 23, 1983.

This picture grab from previously unseen 16mm cinefilm was shot inside an Area 51 hangar. It depicts an ex-Syrian Air Force MiG-17F Fresco C. The highly classified series of evaluations conducted on this particular aircraft by AFSC's 6513th Test Squadron "Red Hats" was code-named Have Drill. To enable these pilots to log flight time on type, this aircraft was redesignated YF-113A (during the same period, another MiG-17F Fresco C was redesignated YF-114C in Have Ferry.) The odd designation for the F-117 was similarly concocted to enable pilots to record flight time in their Air Force logs without uncleared administrators becoming aware of Senior Trend. Note the Israeli Air Force pilot, center. (Paul F. Crickmore collection)

On October 25, 1983, the CTF reached a major milestone when Lt-Col Tackabury dropped the first full-scale weapon, an Mk-84 bomb, from aircraft 782. Two days later Tom Morganfeld dropped the first GBU-10. Finally, on October 28, 1983, the USAF was able to declare that the 4450th Tactical Group at Tonopah had reached IOC.

At the end of November 1984, aircraft 784 was dismantled at Area 51 and flown back to Burbank in the belly of a C-5. The operational shortcomings of a visual targeting system had long been appreciated. Thus, when 784 next flew from Area 51, on September 4, 1985, it was equipped with an LO radar system. On completing its final flight in this configuration on December 12, every aspect of the system had been evaluated in 34 sorties – the RCS of the antenna and radome, its ability to perform the ground-mapping task, and threat evaluation during system operation. Those interviewed who were involved in the program have remarked that the system was incredibly stealthy, however it was not deployed on the fleet for reasons of cost and on the basis that stealth, as a concept, had yet to prove itself operationally.

The F-117's fuel system was originally designed to retain fuel in the wings for as long as possible. This was thought to significantly lower in-flight loads, as the aircraft's center of gravity (CG) was positioned further aft, thereby leading to an extended airframe life. As flight-testing progressed, it was determined that elevon control power was less than predicted, with the aircraft becoming increasingly more difficult to manage at higher AOAs when configured with high-aft CG settings. To regain this loss of control power, FSD-1 was grounded between December 21, 1983 and January 4, 1984, during which time wing leading-edge extensions were added. During nine subsequent flights in this configuration, the modification was judged to have achieved its stated objectives; however, the USAF again decided not to modify the exterior of production aircraft. Instead, fuel sequencing was changed, and wing fuel was used first, thereby avoiding degraded elevon control suffered during high alpha maneuvers and aft CG conditions. Subsequently, the structural engineers decided that, in any event, flying the aircraft in aft CG conditions made little difference to increased airframe life.

Aircraft 824 underwent a series of climatic tests at Eglin AFB, Florida. It is seen here being brought down to subzero temperatures, having first been sprayed with water. (Lockheed Martin via Tony Landis)

An additional responsibility carried out by Lockheed test pilots was to complete all functional check flights (FCFs) for each F-117 as they arrived at Area 51, prior to being commissioned by the USAF. The first production aircraft due to be received in this way was 785; like all F-117s, it was airlifted to the test area via a C-5 Galaxy, reassembled, and then subjected to various ground checks before, on April 20, 1982, company test pilot Bob Riedenauer advanced the throttles to take the aircraft on its first flight. Aircraft 785 rotated as planned, but immediately after liftoff everything went horribly wrong. The nose yawed violently; it then pitched up, and completed a snap roll that left it on its back before impacting the ground. It was nothing short of a miracle that Riedenauer survived; the F-117, however, was totally wrecked. A post-accident investigation established that the pitch and yaw rate gyro inputs to the flight control computer had been cross-wired – result: as the aircraft rotated, the computer's interpretation of events was that of an uncommanded yaw departure. Its "restorative" action therefore was to apply rudder. This, however, caused a real yaw departure, which, to the computer, was perceived as pitch. A full-up elevons response was therefore communicated to the flight control surfaces, resulting in what so easily could have been a fatal accident. Riedenauer suffered two broken legs and other injuries that ended his test pilot career. A production, performance, and quality audit was initiated by Lockheed, after which the gyro connectors were redesigned to physically prevent misinstallation.

Interest in this revolutionary aircraft was also expressed by the USN, and during the latter part of October 1984 Lt-Col Kenny Linn and Lt-Col Ken Grubbs flew 783 and 782 for a total of 11.4 hours evaluating the F-117 for carrier operations. Afterwards, Linn would comment, "Unremarkably, it wasn't suitable at that time for CV [aircraft carrier] use, although it had quite nice handling characteristics in the pattern, landing speeds were too high and the sink rate limitations were too low. The F-117A had not been built as a CV aircraft and it was not going to turn into one overnight".

Not all flights progressed seamlessly through the test card, however, as Maj John Beesley discovered early on the afternoon of September 25, 1985. Shortly into the sortie, and following a pull-up maneuver at 10,000ft, the left fin completely failed. The incident, which was filmed from a chase plane, ended without further incident, as Beesley retained control of the aircraft

C **SPECIAL F-117 PAINT SCHEMES**

1: Aircraft 782 first had the stars and bars applied to its underside in December 1983 for a ceremonial flyby to celebrate a change of command within the F-117 CTF from Roger Moseley to Paul Tackabury. Over the years it had several different paint schemes applied, including a repeat of this scheme in October 2005 to mark the retirement of the F-117 fleet.
2: The F-117 JTF was unofficially known as the "Baja Scorpions." As the test group was located in a complex at the south end of Area 51, other site occupants referred to them as the "South Enders." From this was derived Baja – Spanish, loosely, for south. When one day a scorpion was found and captured in one of the hangars, it was decided that the scorpion image would be aptly symbolic as, like the F-117, it could strike without warning. In 1986 the test team applied a "Baja Scorpions" logo to the underside of aircraft 782. The diameter of the orange disc fell just within the outside edges of the two bomb bay doors. Since the aircraft always had their bomb bays open when on the ground, it ensured that senior USAF officers who might have objected to the logo would not be able to see it.
3: Between November 27 and December 3, 1990, aircraft 831 had the Skunk Works logo applied to its underside. On December 6 the aircraft was flown to Area 51 to celebrate the retirement of Ben Rich, the company's president. The Skunk Works paint scheme was removed from the aircraft immediately after the celebrations had ended.

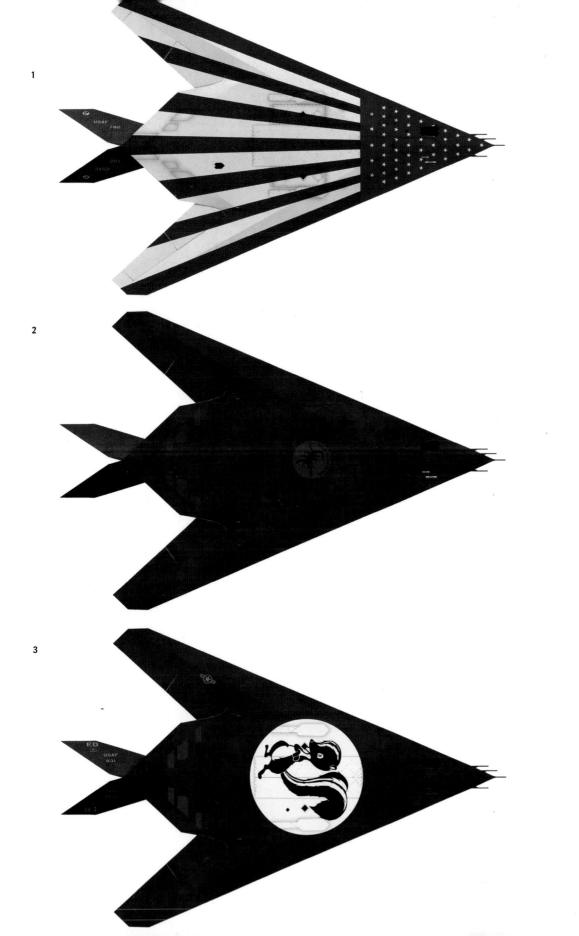

1

2

3

Continued developments in improved radar absorbent coatings required them to be tested before being applied to the entire fleet. Aircraft 783 is seen undertaking such a test at the White Sands RATSCAT facility. (Lockheed Martin via Tony Landis)

and completed a successful recovery back at Area 51. Having saved a highly valuable aircraft, and in so doing demonstrating outstanding pilot skill, Beesley was secretly awarded a Distinguished Flying Cross.

Following the combined USAF–USN raid on Libya in April 1986, the Royal Air Force (RAF) had its chance to evaluate the F-117 by way of a thank you from President Reagan to the Thatcher administration for allowing UK bases to be used to launch the attack. Accordingly, in early May, two RAF test pilots from Boscombe Down – Wing Commander Colin Cruickshanks and Squadron Leader Dave Southwood – deployed in civilian clothes and under conditions of great secrecy to Nevada. Hosted by one of the "operational squadrons," the 4452nd Test Squadron, each pilot accrued about six hours on type before returning to the UK and compiling a highly classified debriefing disc that remained secured in a Boscombe safe for several years before eventually being cleared for destruction.

After aircraft 780 retired, the test fleet was again boosted to five, when in February 1988 aircraft 831 joined their ranks, having completed just 16 flights with the operational wing. Following considerable rework, this aircraft became the testbed for Phase II of the Offensive Capability Improvement Program (OCIP), which incorporated updates to improve pilot situational awareness and reduce workload.

Since the time of the conceptual Have Blue program, Area 51 had served as host for low-observability flight-test operations, but, as elements of stealth ventured out from the Black World, it became possible to move the operation to a more amenable site. So it was that on April 1, 1992, Det 5 relocated to Site 7 at Plant 42, Palmdale and became the 410th Flight Test Squadron (FLTS), with the first Senior Trend test sortie (a weapons evaluation test) being flown from the base by Jim Thomas in aircraft 784 on April 23, 1992.

TECHNICAL SPECIFICATIONS

Stealth features

The F-117 design was based upon the requirement to produce a tactical, survivable interdictor. Data used to help formulate the design was based upon assumptions commensurate with a NATO/Soviet–Warsaw Pact confrontation. Therefore, the principal radar types to be deceived in order to execute the mission and significantly enhance survivability were airborne intercept, surface-to-air missile (SAM), and radar-directed anti-aircraft artillery (AAA), which typically operate on a wavelength of between 3 and 10cm. The physics of radar scattering is largely dependent upon the relationship of size of the radar wavelength versus the physical size of its target. The above decimetric and centimetric band radars fall within an area known as the optical scattering regime, and it is within this regime that an aircraft's shape can be designed in such a way as to precisely control the magnitude and direction of radar reflections. However, the scale of the aeronautical challenge faced by the design team to manufacture an aircraft with "an explicit operational advantage," capable of producing an RCS lower by several orders of magnitude than any current conventional aircraft, is perfectly demonstrated by the radar equation, which basically states that "detection range is proportional to the fourth root of the radar cross section." Therefore, in order to reduce detection range by a factor of ten, it is necessary to reduce the target aircraft's RCS by a factor of 10,000 or 40 dBs.

Having established an overall shape that meets the stated RCS criteria, it then becomes necessary to consider other aspects of an aircraft's design that will impact on these values. The engine inlet of the F-117 is positioned above the wing, and the inlet duct curves very slightly down to the compressor, thereby providing it with an element of shielding. Further reductions in RCS values are achieved by placing a grid over the inlet, the

This chart depicts the physics of radar scattering, which is dependent upon the relationship between the size of a radar's wavelength versus the physical size of its target. In the Raleigh scattering regime, the wavelength is of greater or similar size to its target; therefore, the size of the reflection is proportional to the actual size of the target. Entering the resonant scattering regime, the wavelength is smaller and of comparable size to the target; here the size of the reflection fluctuates strongly with wavelength and the aspect of the target relative to the radar head. Finally, as we move into the optical scattering regime and wavelength is reduced still further, the actual shape of the target can be used to control both the size and direction of the reflections. Hence the effectiveness of the F-117's design when pitted against target acquisition radars that operate in the decimetric and centimetric wavebands, where typical wavelengths are a tenth to a hundredth the size of the key shaping features of the target. (Dr Carlo Kopp, editor-in-chief, *Air Power Australia*).

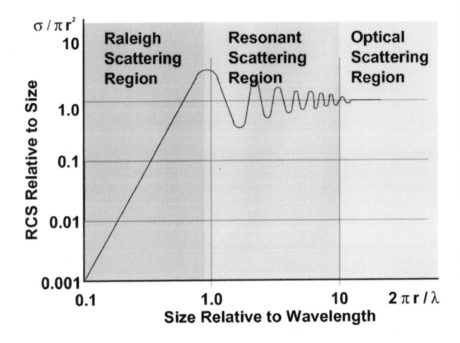

Airframe 777 was initially used as a structural test article. On completion of these tests the airframe was modified and a 53in. hole was cut into the fuselage to enable a rotation device to be installed before undertaking RCS pole tests (Lockheed Martin via Tony Landis)

top of which is angled back from the lower edge with a further nose–aft sweep applied, to reflect radar energy away from the nose-on aspect. Radar-absorbent material (RAM) is also applied to the grid so that the entire unit functions as a solid metal facet. Ice encrustation was never an issue with Have Blue, as it was purely a research aircraft and could therefore be flown in a selective manner. The F-117A, however, was an all-weather aircraft, and icing was a major issue that could affect the air data system and the inlet grids. Problems with the latter became particularly acute if ice bridged across the front grids, thus significantly reducing airflow to the engines. Several approaches to alleviate the issue were examined; however, it was finally decided to use glycol spray in conjunction with a simple windscreen wiper blade which, when not operating, tucked away inside a box below the inlet. In operation, it covers about 80 percent of the inlet area – the remainder is easily digested by the engine.

An aircraft's cockpit is a major source of generating unwanted signal returns, including the pilot's head. To prevent radar energy reflecting back from numerous corner reflectors, the F-117A's cockpit windows were metalized. They worked much like metalized sunglasses, thus allowing the pilot to see out, but to all other intents performing as a faceted panel in relation to electromagnetic radiation, reflecting energy away from its source.

For target acquisition, the F-117A had a system known as IRADS. Unique to Senior Trend, its hardware consists of two external elements: a unit mounted in the upper nose section, known as the FLIR unit, and a DLIR unit, located in the underside of the aircraft's nose section. Completely self-contained, the system enabled the pilot to perform nighttime recognition designation of targets for his guided weapons without recourse to the telltale, electromagnetic radiation emissions associated with radar. Mounted in turrets, which in turn were located in commodious cavities, these units required apertures that were able to pass infrared and laser energy out and back, but were opaque to radar. These criteria were satisfied by utilizing a high-tensile, fine-wire screen.

Other considerations

In addition to producing a low RCS, the F-117A designers also paid good attention to reducing electromagnetic emissions and infrared radiation from the aircraft's hot parts. An important feature of low observability design is that, in general, the differing observable disciplines are mutually inclusive; if something is good for reducing radar returns, it is often found to be good for reducing infrared returns and vice versa. It was appropriate to shield the exhaust nozzle for both radar and infrared reasons. The high aspect-ratio nozzle design was selected to minimize these returns, and also had the effect of increasing the surface area of the exhaust wake, which rapidly increased its cooling (good for both radar and infrared). This also increased the acoustic frequencies, thus attenuating sound to a far greater extent than if exhausted through a conventional, circular nozzle. One area of partial conflict was the platypus bill-shaped shield, behind the exhaust nozzle. This reduced direct radar reflections and infrared emissions from the exhaust nozzle at the expense of generating some infrared radiation from the shield itself. However, because the vast majority of detectors and anti-aircraft weapons were located below the aircraft, it was elected to allow this radiation to be seen from above.

The F-117's faceted air data probes are of unique configuration. Total pressure is measured from a single orifice at the tip of each probe. Orifices on the left and right cheek of each front facet measure differential pressure to determine angle of sideslip (beta). Angle-of-attack (alpha) is resolved by differential pressure taken from ports situated in the upper and lower front facets, while static pressure measurements are collected from four small orifices located on each probe's side facet, further downstream. (Paul F. Crickmore)

Operational analysis

Working on the premise that all the RCS goals had been met, the aircraft would now leave attack radars "blind" to its presence. The next phase of the operational analysis considered optimum speed and altitude in order to achieve accurate weapon delivery. It was soon determined that flying at supersonic speed did not enhance survivability. Indeed, flying at high subsonic speeds actually increased survivability by reducing a defender's ability to detect the aircraft using infrared systems. Therefore, it was decided that the platform would be powered by non-afterburning engines, which also reduced airframe temperatures, further lowering its IR signature.

Flying at treetop height and 500kts does not leave much time to acquire a target; moreover, it places the attacking aircraft within range of many more weapons systems. At the other extreme, maintaining similar knots equivalent airspeed (KEAS) at 35,000ft provides the aircraft with greater target acquisition time, but comes at the expense of delivery accuracy. Optimum weapon effectiveness was achieved by placing the aircraft at medium altitude. For a subsonic aircraft touting a modest performance envelope, the latter would be utter suicide – but not for a stealth aircraft.

The amount of "stealth" required to enhance survivability depends upon the "detection zone." Therefore, with the aircraft maintaining high subsonic speeds, a successful missile attack from the flank would require the weapon to undertake a tight, "high-g" turn, a maneuver still outside the envelope of most systems. From the rear, hopefully the aircraft would have already hit its target and be returning home, thereby placing the missile in a catch-up situation. Directly above and below the aircraft are zones of almost negligible

This graph illustrates the relationship between directional stability with increasing speed (Mach) and AOA on the F-117 – the combined effects requiring a fly-by-wire solution to retain control of the aircraft. (Lockheed Martin)

UNAUGMENTED AIRFRAME CHARACTERISTICS
(CLEAN AIRCRAFT)

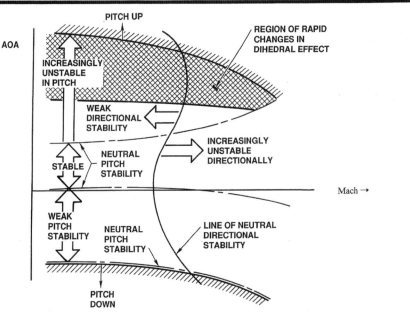

importance. However, the aspect that presents the defender with the greatest chance of a successful intercept is the frontal zone. If the threshold of detection, by radars using wavelengths of between 3 and 10cm, can be foiled to a point where the aircraft is just one minute's flying time (about ten miles) from the radar head, then there is a good chance of avoiding a successful intercept. Therefore, by pulling all these strands together, an F-117, flying at an altitude of 12,000ft and 500kts, will achieve that one-minute detection goal parameter by being at its most "stealthy," head on, 25 degrees look-down, and 25 degrees look-up.

Although the F-117 looked radically different externally, internally many of its subsystems were off-the-shelf items that can be found in other more conventional, non-stealthy platforms. It was powered by two General Electric F404-GE-F1D2 non-afterburning turbofans. The aircraft was 63ft 9in. long, had a span of 43ft 4in., stood 12ft 5in. to the top of its closed canopy, and boasted a modest wing area 912.7 square feet. Low observability necessitated a leading-edge sweep that was completely unbroken from nose to wingtip, of 67.3 degrees. The aircraft's empty weight (including unusable fuel, oil, and pilot) was 29,500lb, which increases to 52,500lb at max takeoff weight – this figure includes 5,000lb of ordnance. On the ground, the F-117 stood on a tricycle undercarriage that had a main wheel track of 14ft 3in.

Powerplant

The two axial-flow turbofan engines each produce a maximum thrust of 10,540lb when uninstalled. However, the way in which the exhaust plumb is ducted through the slotted exit nozzle, in order to reduce its IR signature, reduces the available power down to 9,040lb when installed in the aircraft. The engine's three-stage, low-pressure compressor fan, and the seven-stage high-pressure compressor, are each driven by single-stage turbines. Both the first- and second-stage high-pressure compressor stator blades are variable.

The F-117's General Electric F404 turbofan engines differed from those installed in the McDonnell Douglas F/A-18 as they were not equipped with afterburner. They were designated F404-GE-F1D2. (USAF)

Air bled from the fourth-stage compressor is used by the engine anti-ice system, while variable geometry inlet guide vanes (IGVs) mounted in front of both the fan and compressor direct the flow of inlet air to achieve optimum engine operation. Non-continuous engine ignition is provided by a single ignite. An engine electronic control unit (ECU) and main fuel control (MFC) provide coordinated engine operation.

An engine accessory gearbox, driven by the compressor shaft, drives the oil pump, engine alternator, main fuel pump and main fuel control, together with an airframe-mounted accessory drive (AMAD). Left and right engine blow-in doors are located in the upper surfaces of the engine inlet ducts. The spring-loaded doors are hinged to open whenever the aircraft's speed is less than approximately 0.55 Mach to allow supplementary air to enter the inlet duct. The doors close progressively as the aircraft accelerates and are fully closed at about 0.55 Mach. No action is required of the pilot to open, close, or regulate the position of the doors.

Fuel and oil system

The engine fuel system provides a continuous fuel supply to the combustor manifolds and fan and compressor variable actuators. Fuel is fed into the engine fuel system through a single inlet connection to the main fuel pump. A portion of the main fuel output is routed to the ECU for cooling. After passing through the main fuel pump, fuel is routed into the MFC and then flows into the combustor manifolds and main fuel nozzles. Each engine is equipped with a self-contained oil system.

There are eight fuel tanks in the F-117A and all are filled using a single-point pressure system or the air refueling system. Fuel is contained within the fuselage above the weapons bay and aft of the weapons bay. The tanks are left and right of the aircraft's centerline and are divided into separate compartments. On each side, the forward compartments comprise the forward transfer tank, each with a usable capacity of 2,700lb; the next compartments comprise the engine feed tank with a usable capacity of 2,400lb; and the remaining compartments comprise the aft transfer tanks, each consisting of 1,900lb of usable capacity. Fuel is also carried in each wing, between the front and rear beams outboard to the elevon actuator bay, and they supply 2,100lb of usable capacity each, thus providing a total usable capacity of 18,200lb or 2,800 US gallons of JP-4 or NATO F-40 fuel.

Normally, the left feed tank supplies fuel to the left engine and the right feed tank to the right engine. Each feed tank has two AC-driven boost pumps. The aft boost pump mounted inside a sump tank delivers fuel at higher pressure to the engine feed and during negative g and/or inverted flight. The forward boost pump supplies fuel in the event of an aft boost pump failure. Fuel is not used to trim the aircraft as this is achieved aerodynamically, using control surface position. However, a controlled fuel burn sequence is utilized to maintain the CG, within limits. A high level of redundancy is built into the fuel transfer system, with each boost pump capable of supplying full fuel-flow demands for both engines; should the boost pumps fail, fuel is fed to the engines by gravity. Wing tank fuel is transferred into the fuselage, then the forward and aft transfers push fuel into the feeds.

A fuel pressurization system utilizes conditioned engine bleed air from the environmental control system to conduct an inert agent (Halon) through a vent box and into the air spaces above the tanks.

An air refueling receptacle and its slipway is mounted within the upper fuselage dry bay in the forward transfer tanks and on the aircraft centerline. The receptacle is hydraulically powered and electrically controlled; when actuated, it rotates to the open position. Boom connect provides a secure intercom link with the tanker. Typical off-load fuel flow rates are 2,000lb per minute from a KC-135 and 3,000lb per minute from a KC-10.

Ignition system

Each ignition system contains an independent engine-mounted alternator, an ignition exciter, and a single igniter. Engine start is achieved by moving the throttle from off to idle; this turns on the ignition. In order for the alternator to produce enough power for the plug to cause engine ignition, the engine must be spun above 10 percent RPM. Once this has been achieved, the ignition system remains firing until engine power increases above 45 percent, after which it automatically cuts off (idle power is usually between 62 and 64 percent). In the event of a flame-out, sensors within the engine detect a pressure drop; as the engine winds down below 45 percent, the ignition system again cuts in and remains in operation until engine RPM drops below 10 percent, at which point the system becomes powerless.

Each engine is controlled by a throttle, mounted on the left console, with detents at OFF, IDLE, and MIL. The OFF position terminates engine ignition and fuel flow. The IDLE position commands minimum unified fuel control (UFC) thrust and is used for all ground starts and air starts. From IDLE to MIL, the throttle controls the output of the engine.

An engine can be started by pressurized air supplied through an external connection; from the other operating engine; or from the integral auxiliary power unit (APU). This air is supplied to the air turbine starter (ATS) on the AMAD, which provides cranking for engine start. The engine starting system, self-contained when used with the integral pressurized air starting system (PASS), can provide pressurized air for starting the APU, which then supplies adequate air flow to the ATS for engine start.

Hydraulics

Hydraulic power is supplied by two separate systems: the primary Utility Hydraulic System, and the primary Flight Hydraulic System. Each is then divided into secondary systems, designated A and B, which thereby produce Utility Hydraulic A, Utility Hydraulic B, Flight Hydraulic A, and Flight Hydraulic B. Should a leak develop, a valve sensing a decreasing reservoir level shuts off secondary system A of the affected Utility or Flight hydraulic system. If the leakage continues, secondary system A is restored prior to a shutdown of secondary system B.

The Flight Hydraulic System is powered by two hydraulic pumps, one mounted on the AMAD of each engine. If one engine is shut down, flight hydraulic power continues to be supplied by the flight hydraulic system pump powered by the operating engine. This same system is mirrored to produce

Ed Lovick designed the so-called "egg crate" over the engine inlets. At high frequencies, the grid acted like waveguides. It was manufactured from fibreglass covered with resistive coatings. The latter increased and became increasingly conductive as the radar wave progressed to the rear of the grid. The effect resulted in the inlets blending into the surrounding absorber-coated metal surfaces. Lovick had first used his innovative invention on vent openings on the underside of the A-12. (Paul F. Crickmore)

Extended on their trapeze units, Lt-Col William "Brad" O'Connor is pictured with a pair of live GBU-27s prior to embarking on an operational mission during Operation *Allied Force*. (Lt-Col Brad O'Connor)

utility hydraulic power. The two flight hydraulic systems each power three separate control surfaces for survivability. This is further backed up by Utility B. Utility A provides the muscle for all other hydro-powered equipment on the aircraft – air refueling door, nosewheel steering, APU exhaust door, wipers, landing gear, weapons bay doors, trapeze, and wheel brakes. With the APU operating, the emergency power unit (EPU) can provide emergency hydraulic power to the Flight Hydraulic System when manually selected.

The landing gear is electrically controlled and hydraulically operated. All three undercarriage legs retract forward, thereby providing a freefall auxiliary extension capability. Nosewheel steering is mechanically controlled via the rudder pedals and is electro-hydraulically powered with two steering ranges. The system automatically engages when the nose strut is compressed by the weight of the aircraft and provides a steering range of 10 degrees left or right, but, by pressing and holding the nosewheel steering button on the control stick, the range is increased to 45 degrees left or right.

Electrical system

The generators are the same as those used on the F/A-18. The AC equipment consists of a 115/200 volt, three-phase, 400 Hertz system, supplied by two 30/40 kVA constant-speed generators, one mounted on each engine. DC power is then obtained from two AC-to-DC converters that supply DC power to the left and right main DC buses, the left and right essential buses, and the battery bus. Emergency power is provided by a 5 kVA auxiliary generator, which is powered by the EPU, driven by APU exhaust gases. In the event of a multiple generator and EPU failure, batteries provide power to the flight control system for approximately ten minutes, during which time an immediate landing is essential, if a complete failure of the fly-by-wire flight control system and subsequent loss of the aircraft is to be avoided.

Flight control system

As already discussed, the external shape of the F-117 was determined by the requirement to meet a specific set of LO criteria. Its CG locations were determined by the aircraft's structure, engines, fuel, and mission equipment located within the airframe. As a consequence, the F-117 is an aircraft of unusual aerodynamic configuration, high dihedral effect, and with a large operating range of CG travel. At forward CG – full payload and 4,000lb of fuel or less – its unaugmented stability and control characteristics are similar to those of a more conventional aircraft. However, at the aft CG position – no payload, and full wing, feed, and aft transfer fuel tanks – the aircraft would be unflyable without significant artificial stability augmentation through the flight control system (FCS). Critical to providing an effective FCS is the accurate collection of air data. This is achieved utilizing a unique, four-probed, pitot-static system. It consists of four similar subsystems with each nose-mounted probe supplying static pressure signals and total pressure, alpha (AOA), and beta (sideslip) differential pressure signals to the flight control computer (FLCC). The C probe supplies total and static pressures to the air data computer (ADC) that provides data via the dual-data multiplex bus to the W-weapons system computer (W-WSC), for weapon delivery calculations. The B probe supplies total and static pressures to the pilot's standby instruments, the latter being completely independent of the static ports supplying signals to the FLCC. These standby instruments, located on the left side of the instrument panel, include the vertical velocity indicator, altimeter, and the airspeed indicator.

When the aircraft is on the ground, DC power is used to heat the pitot/static manifolds and associated plumbing to prevent condensation from collecting; once airborne, the probes are heated to prevent icing. The four-channel, computer-controlled fly-by-wire system hydraulically positions the control surfaces on pilot command. The aircraft is controlled in pitch and roll through the deflection of inboard and outboard elevons. Directional control is provided through the two movable fins. Six integrated dual servo actuators power the control surfaces, one for each elevon and one for each fin. The primary flight controls and trim in all three axes are mechanized as a quadruple-redundant command augmentation system with no mechanical backup. The pilot controls the pitch and roll axes through the conventional movable center stick; similarly, directional control is accomplished with conventional rudder pedals. The stick and rudder pedal positions are converted to quadruple electrical signals, which are then compared with acceleration and rate feedback in the FLCC. This in turn processes and

There are always compromises to be made in aircraft design, as is graphically demonstrated here, in relation to pressure distribution over the surface of a faceted wing (A) compared to that of a conventional wing (B). Lift generated on the leading edge of the faceted wing's elevon, together with the pressure spike on the elevon's underside trailing edge, combine to necessitate an extremely robust attachment assembly. (Lockheed Martin)

FACETED SURFACE PRESSURE DISTRIBUTION

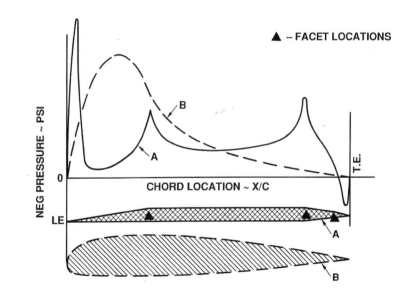

▲ – FACET LOCATIONS

NEG PRESSURE ~ PSI

CHORD LOCATION ~ X/C

T.E.

modifies these signals and generates the appropriate flight control surface command signals. These signals are then transmitted to the triple-redundant electro-hydraulic servo valves in the hydraulic integrated servo actuators that control the individual surfaces. Automatic and manual trim modes are provided for both pitch and yaw axes; however, roll trim can only be achieved manually.

The FLCC contains several limiters that automatically restrict pitch axis maneuvering to prevent exceeding specified AOA and load factors. For example, full aft stick always commands positive 7g, but the positive AOA limiter overrides the pilot input and restricts the load factor to a lesser value if required by the prevailing conditions. Similarly, full forward stick always commands negative 2g; however, since there is no negative AOA limiter, the pilot must closely monitor such inputs below 200kts. To further safeguard against exceeding the AOA for any given set of flight conditions, a warning system is fitted which provides the pilot with a variable audio tone through the earphones. A mechanized voice-alert warning system provides warnings to the pilot if the Mach/airspeed limit is exceeded or if the aircraft dips below its minimum en-route altitude.

Autopilot

The autopilot system has both dual-channel monitored operation and single-channel operation, and provides roll and pitch attitude hold, heading hold, Mach or altitude hold, and navigation steering capabilities. When engaged, the maximum pitch and roll angles that will be maintained are +/- 30 degrees and +/- 70 degrees respectively.

Flight instruments

Electromechanical flight instruments are provided as a backup to flight data displayed on the multipurpose display indicators (MDI). These include an attitude director indicator (ADI), horizontal situation indicator (HSI), altimeter, airspeed indicator, and a vertical velocity indicator grouped to the left side of the instrument panel. AOA and beta (side-slip) indicators are located either side of the upper center panel, and a radar altimeter and turn-and-slip indicator is positioned on the right side of the instrument panel, together with the engine performance instruments and fuel quantity gage.

Displays

The F-117's cockpit is dominated by four major displays: a head-up display (HUD), situated at the top center of the instrument panel; a sensor display below the HUD; and two MDIs located either side of the sensor display.

The HUD combines real-world cues and flight direction symbology. Focused at infinity, it creates the illusion that the symbols are superimposed on the real world. Although the HUD is primarily attack orientated and has specific formats for the various attack modes, it also displays basic flight data, including instrument landing system (ILS) steering data to support ILS approaches.

The two MDIs were identical and displayed a variety of general flight and system information, and, under certain conditions, image data. Each MDI had five multifunction switches along each of its four sides. Eight MDI display formats were driven by the WSC, each with variations depending upon the state of the system and each with a specific set of associated switch functions. These formats were grouped into two sets. One set, referred to as the HSD group, consisted of the status (STAT) display, the stores management display (SMD), the horizontal situation display (HSD), and the tactical plot (TP) display. The second set, known as the VSD group, consisted of the basic test display, the SMS (stores management system) test display and the vertical situation display (VSD). Typically, the left MDI was used to display one of the HSD group formats whilst the right MDI had the VSD format displayed in order to provide good head-down attitude and steering data – however, any format from either group could be displayed on either or both MDIs. Upon entry to an attack mode, the SMD was automatically displayed upon the MDI that had the HSD group selected.

Avionics integration

The integrated avionics configuration of the F-117 has been carefully selected to maximize the effectiveness of the aircraft without compromising the operational advantages gained from the application of LO technology. Passive operation in the infrared portion of the spectrum was selected as the most viable sensing method. As its name implies, the infrared acquisition designation system (IRADS) incorporates target ranging, designation, and tracking capabilities. A self-contained navigational capability is provided by a highly accurate inertial navigation system (INS) and other aids, including TACAN (tactical air navigation); an ILS has also been provided for use in non-hostile areas. The endgame of these highly integrated systems is to provide single-pilot management and control of a complex aircraft and its mission.

Senior Trend's original avionics package was orientated around three Delco M362 F computers with 32k words of 16-bit core memory, as used in the F-16. Interconnected via a dual-redundant MIL-STD-1553 data bus, the Weapon Delivery Computer was the executive, providing overall control, as well as updating cockpit displays, performing weapon delivery calculations, and controlling data distribution. The Navigation Control Computer performed all navigation and control functions, including inertial measurement, navigation, and flight director steering, as well as position update, TACAN, and ILS interface, among others. The third computer provided control and data processing for a supplementary system, and in addition provided backup, should either of the other two computers fail.

Air Force operating procedures required the left CMDI to display primary flight data information at all times. The right CMDI could also display primary flight data; however, operational aircraft used this display for the HSI, moving map, or access to status and maintenance pages. (Lockheed Martin)

Once mission planning has been completed, details are fed into the mission data processing system (MDPS), which is then downloaded into the expanded data transfer module (EDTM). The latter is a transportable computer memory module that is loaded with mission-unique data and is carried by the pilot out to his aircraft. The EDTM is then inserted into the expanded data transfer module interface unit (EDTMIU). During preflight this mission-unique data is loaded into the aircraft's mission computers through a high-speed bus. As the Honeywell SPN-GEANS INS navigates the aircraft to the target area, the computer system cues the IR system to the target. Placing the crosshairs of his sensor display on the target and various offsets, the pilot refines the aiming point; laser then designates the target and consents for weapon release. The Weapon Delivery Computer simultaneously performs relevant ballistic calculations, based upon the weapon to be dispatched, together with inertial navigation system (INS) and IR inputs. Weapons release then occurs via the SMS at the appropriate time.

The IRADS is built by Texas Instruments (now Raytheon). As mentioned previously, two turrets are mounted in "contour" to conform to set RCS criteria. The target is initially acquired by the FLIR unit, located in the top turret. It is then tracked by a video camera and displayed on the IR targeting screen in the cockpit. As the "look angle" increases, the target is "handed off" to the DLIR, housed in the lower turret. Because the two turrets are identical (and interchangeable), the video picture received by the DLIR has to be inverted electronically when displayed to the pilot, thus enabling the image to remain top side up. Despite many initial problems, the system is capable of tracking the target throughout dive-toss-type deliveries, where it could be subjected to as many as three handoffs and air loads of 4 positive-g during loft maneuvers.

Antenna systems

Fixed flush and retracting blade antennas are installed on the aircraft to provide transmission and reception of necessary signals for operational requirements. The UHF communication system (AN/ARC-164V) consists of two retractable antennae, one upper and the other lower, and provides

D F-117 WEAPONS

1. GBU-12, a 500lb weapon using the Paveway II laser guidance system
2. GBU-10, a 1,000lb bomb using Paveway II
3. GBU-27. A bunker-busting 2,000lb weapon using the updated Paveway III laser guidance system
4. EGBU-27. The Enhanced Guided Bomb Unit incorporated a GPS unit in addition to Paveway III, enabling the weapon to be dropped with pinpoint accuracy through cloud. During Operation *Iraqi Freedom*, F-117s dropped 98 EGBU-27s in 82 attacks
5. SUU-20. The SUU-20 practice bomb carrier was used extensively during stateside training sorties
6. MXU-648 baggage pod - used to carry the pilots personal equipment during TDY deployment away from home-plate.
7. AGM-158 JASSM. Following later tests the F-117 was cleared to use the Lockheed AGM-158 JASSM, the Boeing JDAM guidance system and Raytheon AGM-154 JSOW, but none of these were used operationally before the program was canceled.
8. Mk 84 2,000lb bomb fitted with the JDAM guidance kit, which converts "dumb" bombs into GPS precision-guided munitions
9. AGM-154 JSOW Joint Standoff Weapon
10. B61 free-fall nuclear weapon
11. B57 free-fall nuclear weapon
12. The F-117's unique hydraulic weapons trapeze

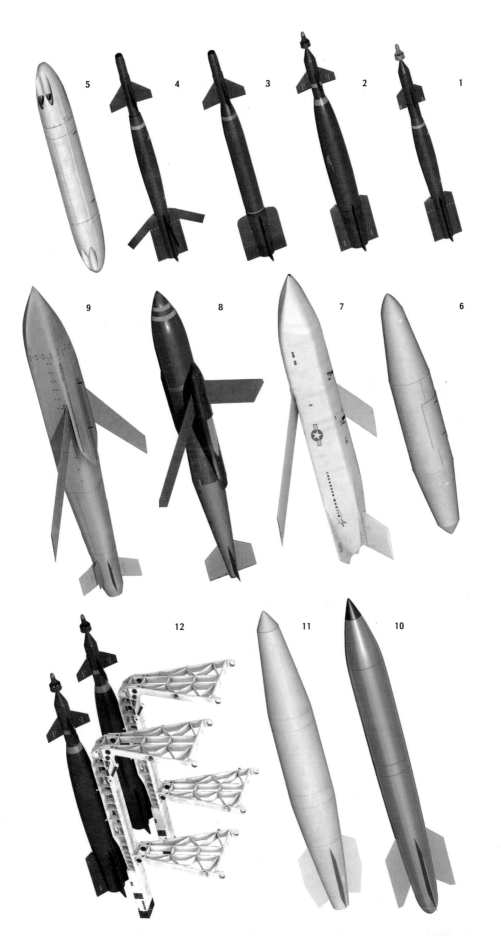

Construction of all 60 F-117s took place within the Skunk Works facilities at Burbank. Final assembly (as seen here) was conducted within buildings 309 and 310. (Lockheed Martin)

amplitude-modulated two-way radio communication with other similarly equipped aircraft or ground stations. With a normal line-of-sight range of 220nmi, communications can be conducted on one of 20 preset channels, or on any one of 7,000 manually selected frequencies.

The Have Quick (HQ) system provides normal and anti-jamming mode UHF comms by frequency hopping. Because the particular frequency in use at any instant depends on a precise time of day, all participating HQ UHF radios must have synchronized clocks. For additional security, the system also uses a word of the day (WOD), consisting of up to six three-digit segments and one of three frequency nets: A-Nets, Sectionalized A-Nets, and T-Nets – the former are used in operational situations.

The F-117 is also equipped with a secure voice communications system (KY-58) which is used with the UHF comms system to provide normal (plain) and cipher (coded) communications. The aircraft is also provided with an identification system, namely the AN/APX-101. This system also comprises two upper and lower retractable antennae and five operating modes – 1, 2, and 4 for tracking and identification purposes, and modes 3/A and C for tracking and altitude reporting.

Environmental control system

The environmental control system (ECS) air-conditioning and pressurization functions to provide temperature-controlled, pressure-regulated air for heating, cooling, ventilating, canopy defogging, cockpit pressurization, canopy sealing, g-suit pressurization, fuel tank pressurization, and electronic equipment cooling. Engine bleed air is directed through a turbine compressor and air-to-air heat exchangers where it is cooled by ram air. Conditioned air enters the cockpit, having received signals from temperature sensors and from a manually operated control panel to automatically control the cockpit temperature. Air pressurization is provided by the pressurization system for control/operation of some of the ECS, canopy seal, g-suit and fuel tanks. Pressure in the cockpit is controlled automatically according to a predetermined schedule. A cockpit pressure safety valve relieves pressure if ever the cockpit pressure exceeds ambient pressure by 5.4psi. The canopy seal is inflated/deflated with the mechanical locking/unlocking of the canopy.

Oxygen system

A five-liter liquid oxygen system provides breathing oxygen to a diluter demand oxygen regulator. The regulator provides for selections of normal diluted oxygen and 100 percent oxygen. Oxygen duration varies depending upon altitude, regulator settings, and usage. The emergency oxygen system consists of a high-pressure bottle and a regulator mounted on the side of the ejector seat, and is activated automatically upon ejection or manually by tugging a green ring located on the left side of the seat.

Ejection seat

The pilot of an F-117A sits in an ACES II ejection seat. The mode of operation of this zero-speed, zero-altitude seat depends upon the aircraft's speed and altitude. Seat ejection is initiated by pulling ejection handles on the side of the seat. This retracts the shoulder harness and locks the inertia reel, fires initiators for canopy jettison, and ignites the canopy removal rockets. As the seat leaves the aircraft, lanyards fire two seat-ejection initiators. A rocket catapult propels the seat from the cockpit, and the emergency oxygen is activated. The recovery sequencer selects the correct recovery mode based on pitot-sensor inputs, and ignites the stabilization package and the trajectory divergence rocket. If the ejection sequence was initiated with the aircraft travelling above 250 KIAS (knots indicated airspeed), initiation of the drogue gun for seat stabilization occurs.

Updates

In 1984 the F-117's avionics architecture was the subject of a three-phase Offensive Capability Improvement Program (OCIP). Phase I, the weapon system computational subsystem (WSCS) upgrade program, was initiated to replace the Delco M362Fs with IBM AP-102 MIL-STD-1750A computers. These new units boasted the capability of one million instructions per second and a 16 bit CPU with 128k words of 16-bit memory expandable to 256k – it is a repackaged version of that used in the space shuttle.

The AP-102s are the same in number and address the same disciplines as the Delcos, and are nominally assigned to execute the appropriate operational flight program as the W-WSC, the N-WSC, and the X-WSC. The W-WSC is the system controller and data integrator; it drives the primary displays and provides all the weapon delivery functions, and is therefore a prime computer. The N-WSC provides precision inertial navigation, which, due to the very limited sensors carried by the aircraft, is critical for most missions; therefore, it too is a prime computer. The X-WSC computer can be used as a backup for either of the other two. The increased onboard computational power has made possible a number of new capabilities, the first of these being the successful deployment of the GBU-27 laser-guided bomb (LGB), together with the ability to perform dual bay weapon deliveries.

Phase II of OCIP afforded greater situational awareness, and reduced pilot workload, by allowing a 4D Flight Management System to fly complex profiles automatically that featured speed and time over target (TOT) control. Also included in this phase was the installation of color multipurpose display indicators (CMDI) and a digital tactical situation display or moving map, a new data entry panel, a display processor, an auto-throttle system, and a pilot-activated automatic recovery system (PAARS).

This is the pre-OCIP Phase III F-117 flight simulator. The green-and-white MDIs flanking the centrally mounted IR sensor display were replaced by CMDIs. (Lockheed Martin)

The active liquid crystal display incorporated in the HUD indicates that this is a post-OCIP Phase III F-117 cockpit. (Lockheed Martin)

Two CMDIs replaced the MDIs and perform the same functions in addition to the moving map display, which provides a capability to monitor the aircraft's route of flight, update navigation, view threat locations, and highlight high terrain features. There are two modes of operation: automatic, where the aircraft reference symbol follows the route of flight, and manual, where a switch on the throttle is used to move around the map. Using the two-position map database switch provides a choice of paper map (PMAP), which consists of a digitized database from photocopying maps such as the tactical pilotage chart (TPC), or the DMAP, which consists of a database from the Defense Mapping Agency's digital files. The latter can be altered to meet special needs, such as highlighting certain terrain. A maximum of ten threats at any one time can appear on the map display.

PAARS was installed as a result of the fatal F-117 accidents, where spatial disorientation was a contributing factor. Upon pilot command, the autopilot, even if not engaged, commands the flight control system and auto-throttles, to fly a pre-programmed set of maneuvers, based upon entry attitude and airspeed, to recover the aircraft to straight and level flight.

Phase III of OCIP saw the replacement of the aging SPN-GEANS INS system with a new Honeywell H-423/E ring laser gyro (RLG), which was supplemented by a Rockwell-Collins global positioning system (GPS), thereby giving rise to the title RNIP-plus. The new INS reduces alignment time from 43 minutes for SPN-GEANS to just 9 minutes and considerably enhances overall reliability, increasing the mean time between failures from 400 to 2,000 hours. The H-423 may not boast enhanced accuracy (still believed to be 0.12 nmi/h), however, when used in association with GPS, the system represents a significant advance in navigational accuracy.

Another update addressed communication issues once an operational aircraft had "stealthed up" – retracting antennae and the like made further communication impossible until the aircraft had completed its mission and arrived back at a prearranged contact point and once again extended its antennae. On October 23, 1991, an LO communications study was authorized to identify methods of overcoming such problems. The result was the development of a stealthy antenna that was evaluated between August 31 and November 13, 1992, onboard aircraft 783. The system received full-scale development go-ahead on May 12, 1993, and work to upgrade the entire fleet began just four months later.

Not all programs, however, meet with the same level of success. For example, during Senior Shade II, aircraft 782 was painted light gray. Between July 12 and September 22, 1993, it flew 14 flights, usually in company with 831, also from the 410th Flight Test Squadron, enabling direct comparisons to be made between the effectiveness of the paint scheme. That F-117s remained black is probably an indication of the evaluation's findings.

Yet another attempt to reduce visual acquisition took place over four flights, between July 19 and 22, 1993. Code-named "Senior Spud," aircraft 784 was half-covered in a textured, reflective surface – a modification that met with a similar lack of approval.

Further development work to enhance communications technology got underway in December 1997 with a flight-test project known as IRRCA (Integrated Real-time Information into the Cockpit/Real-time Information Out of the Cockpit for Combat Aircraft). By June 30, 1998, the first phase of the program, "real-time information into the cockpit," had been successfully demonstrated. At the heart of IRRCA is the integration of a real-time symmetric multiprocessor facilitating 1.2 billion instructions per second. As the F-117 receives threat updates from satellite broadcasts, a moving map displays new threats and the processor automatically evaluates the situation. Should analysis of the threat determine that the aircraft is in peril, the processor re-plans the route and displays the option on a new color liquid crystal diode multifunction display. Decision criteria used in the proposed reroute includes threat exposure, flying time, and landing fuel. The pilot can then accept or reject the proposed option. In addition to mission information, text and images also update the pilot on key events and weather. Evaluations carried out by the 410th indicate that the F-117 is capable of reacting to mission updates or target changes and pop-up threats, while still remaining in a stealth configuration. On June 30, 1998, Jim "JB" Brown, lead IRRCA test pilot, flew a 1.2hr simulated combat mission in the dedicated testbed, aircraft 784. During the course of the sortie, a satellite in geosynchronous orbit transmitted a series of encrypted messages to the aircraft via its LO communications antenna. These messages included threat updates, mission updates, text information, and alternative target imagery.

Mission changes provided information for the real-time symmetric multiprocessor to re-plan the mission to an alternative target. This was followed by a text message and photos of the alternative target that enabled Brown to verify the processor's planning results and study target details prior to acquisition and attack. Phase two of the project, "real-time information out of the cockpit," was demonstrated in June 2001. This so-called time critical targeting (TCT) capability was incorporated into the rest of the operational fleet, where it was utilized during Operation *Iraqi Freedom*.

The final, major modification made to the fleet was designated Single Configuration Fleet 7 (SCF 7). The F-117A's revolutionary radar-absorbent

Nicknamed the "Gray Dragon," in December 2003 aircraft 835 was coated in the same materials used on the F-22 Raptor. (Lockheed Martin via Tony Landis)

material (RAM) was one of the most important components of its LO capabilities. At the same time, it represented the highest operations and support (O&S) costs for the stealthy attack jet. In part, this was due to the wide variety of RAM materials that had been developed and applied to individual aircraft during the course of its production run. Ongoing flight-test and design refinements had therefore resulted in an F-117 fleet outfitted with a patchwork of different RAM coating configurations. The goal of the SCF program was to reconfigure the entire F-117 fleet with a single RAM coating configuration, with the expectation of enhancing the RAM of the aircraft's LO system and reducing both the maintenance man-hours and the quantities of LO materials needed. At the same time, improvements to make access panels easier to remove would enhance RCS capabilities and improve maintainability as well. To these ends, the CTF began modifying aircraft s/n 79-10783 with a new RAM coating on March 31, 1998. During the course of the modification, the aircraft's wing tanks, which had been capped off in 1992, were refurbished and made operational. A/C 783 commenced 50 hours of SCF flight evaluations in August, and a second F-117 (s/n 85-0831) began its refurbishment, entering flight-testing in March 1999.

Weapons systems

Conceived before the advent of GPS weapon delivery systems, the F-117 utilized a laser guidance system to mount its stealthy attack. (Paul F. Crickmore)

All weapons carried by the F-117A are secured to a unique, hydraulically lowered trapeze. This dates back to the aircraft's initial design specification, which stipulated that it should be capable of hauling two of any weapon types in the USAF inventory. This being the case, the F-117 is, at least in theory, capable of hauling target-acquiring weapons such as Maverick, AIM-7s, 9s, and 120s; only a limited number of ground tests of the aircraft firing an AIM-9 were completed.

Weapons system integration has already been covered, but it is worth looking here at the development of LGBs, which were used to such devastating effect by the F-117. At IOC, the originally prescribed precision-guided munition for the aircraft was the GBU-10 laser-guided bomb. The weapon employed a 2,000lb Mk-84 body and a Paveway II guidance unit, which was fitted to the nose section. The guidance unit endeavoured to correct the weapon's trajectory via commands sent to four canards, also attached to the forward section of the weapon. This early guidance unit utilized harsh full deflection commands that often led to over-correction; this in turn led to a loss of the weapon's energy and a failure to achieve optimum trajectory. The net result was that, even if the weapon reached its target, it often had a high AOA, low impact velocity, and poor impact angle. A precision guided munitions (PGM) initiative produced a weapon with an improved 2,000lb casing, giving it an enhanced penetration capability – this was designated the BLU-109. Under the code name "Have Hammer," the BLU-109 was married to a new and improved guidance section designated Paveway III; the new weapon was

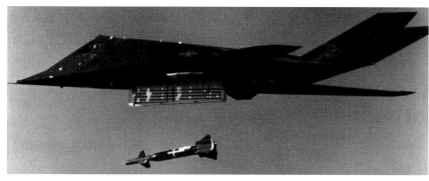

Aircraft 784 is seen here dropping an inert 2,000lb GBU-27 during separation trials. The weapon's release trapeze remained in the bomb bay, to ensure the aircraft retained the lowest possible RCS during the weapon release phase of attack. Note the underwing fairing housing cameras to record weapon separation data. (Lockheed Martin)

designated GBU-27. The first weapon accuracy test was conducted on May 28, 1987, by Jim Dunn flying aircraft 783. The inert weapon scored a direct hit on the target – a 55-gallon barrel, actually splitting it in half! Before the Senior Trend program was terminated, tests and the integration of the Lockheed Martin AGM-158 JASSM Joint Air-to-Surface Standoff Missile), the Boeing JDAM (Joint Direct Attack Munitions), and the Raytheon AGM-154 JSOW (Joint Stand-Off Weapon) were also completed.

OPERATIONAL HISTORY

The Tonopah years

The 4450th Tactical Group was formed on October 15, 1979. Referred to as A-unit, the USAF's first operational F-117 unit was commanded by Col Robert "Burner" Jackson. To preserve security, the unit reported directly to the TAC Director of Operations (DO), instead of a numbered air force. Whilst work on the prototype aircraft continued at Burbank, Jackson began organizing a covert operational base, and it was decided that Tonopah Test Range (TTR) would fit the bill.

Located northwest of Nellis AFB, Nevada, the remote base was already home to another covert outfit – the Red Eagles operating MiGs in project *Constant Peg*. However, to bring the base up to spec a multimillion-dollar construction program was launched, during which the original 6,000ft runway was increased to 12,000ft. Maintenance facilities, a new control tower, fuel and weapon storage areas, as well as permanent housing were also built, together with individual aircraft hangars that were organized into parallel blocks and referred to as canyons.

By early July 1982 the enormous construction program had been completed. Twenty Ling Tempo Vought A-7Ds, including a small number of two-seat A-7Ks, provided a cover story for the unit. These aircraft, based at Nellis AFB, were referred to as P-Unit. Other support elements of the 4450th were given similar oblique and short nicknames, to further conceal their purpose. The 1880th Communication Squadron became C-Unit; Detachment 8 of the 25th Air Weather Squadron was D-Unit; and the 4450th Combat Support Group became E-Unit. The 4450th Test Squadron (established on June 11, 1981) was I-Unit, and Detachment 1 of A-Unit, based at Tonopah, was Q-Unit. In addition to providing the "avionics testing" cover story, the A-7s were used to maintain pilot proficiency until F-117As became available, and were also used as chase aircraft.

Specialist support equipment

The unique characteristics of Senior Trend necessitated the construction of several specialist pieces of support equipment. On September 12, 1985, the go-ahead was given for the production of two air-transportable equipment vans, known as Elvira I and Elvira II. In addition to providing extra maintenance and support equipment, they also incorporated a complete avionics diagnostic system. Both vans were later upgraded to reflect avionics changes to the F-117A fleet, brought about by the OCIP.

In addition to overseeing the construction program, Col Jackson also set about recruiting the initial cadre of pilots, selecting Maj Al Whitney to become the first operational F-117 pilot. The Monday out–Friday back commute from Nellis to Tonopah (a distance of 190 miles) was handled by the civil contractor Key Airlines, operating Boeing 727s (later replaced by Boeing 737s).

Aircraft 787 was the first operational F-117 to be accepted by the USAF, on August 23, 1982, and was joined 11 days later by 786. In September, Detachment 1 of the 4450th was designated the 4452nd Test Squadron. It was while the unit had a complement of just two aircraft that on the night of Friday October 15 Maj Al Whitley conducted his first Senior Trend flight. In so doing, he became the first operational pilot to fly the aircraft.

The F-117 delivery schedule was sporadic, and by the end of 1982 the unit could only boast seven aircraft. Unlike the Senior Trend CTF at Area 51, all Tonopah's F-117 flight activity took place at night. Hangar doors were not opened until one hour after sunset, which put the first scheduled takeoffs at about 1900 hours in winter and 2130 hours in summer. For the first year, flights were restricted to within the Nellis range complex, but as confidence grew, flights were cleared off the range. By the end of 1983, the TTR F-117 fleet had expanded to 12 aircraft.

Col James S. Allen assumed command of the 4450th from Col Bob Jackson on May 17, 1982, and by October 28, 1983, Senior Trend was deemed to have achieved limited initial operational capability (LIOC). Already by the end of 1982, Senior Trend's potential was glaringly apparent to those cleared into the program. Consequently, the procurement plan increased to a total of 57 aircraft (the final total was 59). The impact of this decision created the need for two additional squadrons. As a result, in July 1983 I-Unit "Nightstalkers" was activated, to be followed in October 1985 by Z-Unit "Grim Reapers" (later redesignated the 4450th Test Squadron and the

Hangarage at TTR was in the form of "drive-through" barns grouped in blocks of six. Note the uncompromisingly high, double barbed-wire fencing separated by a well-lit, highly monitored "dead zone" that isolated the flight line, hangars, and other sensitive areas from the rest of the base. (Lockheed Martin)

4453rd Test and Evaluation Squadron respectively). On June 15, 1984, Col Howell M. Estes III became the 4450th's third commander, and on May 5, 1985, he successfully led the unit through its first operational readiness inspection (ORI). Estes handed over command to Col Michael W. Harris on December 6, 1985.

First losses

The bat-like existence of F-117 pilots at this time – sleeping during the day and flying only at night – was both highly demanding and chronically tiring. At 0113 hours on Friday July 11, 1986, in excellent weather and good visibility, Maj Ross E. Mulhare departed Tonopah in aircraft 792. At 0145 hours 792 ploughed into a hillside, killing its pilot. An accident investigation established that at the time of impact, the aircraft was upright, in a steep dive, impacting the ground at "high velocity" with both engines operating at high power settings. There was no indication of a pre-crash fire or that Mulhare had attempted to eject. The prime reason behind this horrific accident was almost certainly pilot fatigue and spatial disorientation.

On April 3, 1987, the 4450th received its fifth commander, Col Michael C. Short. Six months later, on October 14, 1987, Maj Michael C. Stewart died whilst flying 815 under similar circumstances to those of Mulhare. Yet again the accident report failed to clearly determine the cause, but made repeated references to pilot fatigue and disorientation.

Six days after the loss of Maj Stewart, Maj Bruce L. Teagarden (Bandit 222) safely ejected from his A-7D after the aircraft lost power. Unfortunately, the A-7 crashed into the Ramada Inn Hotel, near Indianapolis Airport, killing 9 people. Following a detailed accident investigation, Teagarden was cleared of all culpability. Although publicly acknowledged as being a member of the 4450th, the unit was not known to have any links with Tonopah, ensuring that Senior Trend remained "in the black."

On August 10, 1988, Col Antony J. Tolin took over as wing commander. Just two months later, during the run-up to a presidential election, the Reagan administration requested the Pentagon to schedule a public unveiling event for the F-117. It was a blatant piece of electioneering, infuriating some senior congressmen; consequently the event was delayed until November 10, 1988, one week after the outcome of the election had been decided. On that day, at a Pentagon press conference, Assistant Secretary of Defense J. Daniel Howard held

Aircraft 81-10796 was first flown by Tom Morgenfeld on June 16, 1983 and is seen here in the TTR circuit. One of the minor issues to arise when the F-117 ventured from the "Black World" was serial number duplication. This aircraft is one of six FY 1981 F-117s that required an additional digit adding to its serial number to differentiate it from a batch of F-16A Block 15 Hs carrying the same number. (Lockheed Martin)

up a fuzzy photograph of the F-117, and all the rumors about the "F-19" and its shape were instantly dashed. Releasing the general shape of the aircraft allowed the 4450th to begin daylight flights, which naturally led to sightings being reported. On April 12, 1989, ten were observed flying separately a few miles north of Edwards AFB, and a further six F-117As with their lights were seen adhering to the same route between 2200 hours and 2300 hours that night.

Easing Senior Trend into the "White World" had other positive spinoffs. Gone was the need to shelter the 4450th's covert activity behind a more valid aircraft type. Consequently, in September 1989 the Wing retired its A-7s and instead began operating far more economical AT-38Bs, in the chase/pilot proficiency role. Yet another change followed on October 5, 1989, when the 4450th TG, together with its component squadrons, was redesignated. The parent designation changed to the 37th Tactical Fighter Wing; the 4450th (Nightstalkers) together with the 4451st Test Squadron became the 415th (Nightstalkers) and the 416th (Ghost Riders) respectively. The training unit, the 4453rd (Grim Reapers) Test and Evaluation Squadron, continued its flight training responsibility, but became the 417th (Bandits) Tactical Fighter Training Squadron (TFTS). The historical significance of these unit designations was that they had formed the first US nightfighter squadrons of World War II.

Operation *Just Cause*

By the late 1980s, relations between Panama's military dictator Gen Manuel Noriega and the US had deteriorated after numerous incidents to the point where, on December 15, 1989, Noriega declared a state of war between the two countries. Following an incident in which a US Marine lieutenant was killed by Panamanian Defense Force (PDF) troops, the Bush administration decided to remove Noriega and issued orders to implement Operation *Just Cause* – the code name for a preplanned US invasion of Panama.

In support of the operation, at 1400 hours local time on December 19, 1989, eight F-117s launched from Tonopah (two airborne spares returned following completion of the initial air refueling (AR). The decision to employ the F-117 was based upon its bomb-delivery accuracy; Panama did not possess a radar defense network, so the aircraft's stealth features were irrelevant. The three thousand mile round trip from Tonopah to England AFB, Louisiana, required five ARs and was supported by KC-10s and KC-135s.

Of the six aircraft in the strike package, two were airborne spares, two were tasked with attacking the Rio Hato army base, and the other two were designated to hit Noriega's residences at the Rio Hato beach house and La Escondida mountain resort. In the event, the planned attacks on the dictator's residences were canceled, when intelligence reports indicated that the intended target would not be present at either location. However, Maj Greg Feest, flying aircraft 816, and his wingman Maj Dale Hanner, dropped two 2,000lb GBU-27s in an open field adjacent to the barracks. The purpose of the target selection was to stun and confuse, rather than kill, the sleeping soldiers before they had an opportunity to engage US Rangers parachuting in to occupy the Rio Hato airstrip, 90 seconds after the F-117 strike. However, three hours before the invasion was due to begin, the PDF gained advanced warning of the impending invasion and deployed to the Rio Hato airstrip. In the event, the bombing results were not as effective as had been planned, and several Rangers were killed and more than a dozen wounded in the ensuing firefight before the airfield could be secured. As for

Noriega, having initially taken refuge in a church, he was eventually extradited to Florida. This rather inauspicious combat debut for the F-117 would pale into insignificance, however, just 13 months later.

Operation *Desert Storm*

At 0200 hours (Baghdad time) on August 2, 1990, three Iraqi Republican Guard divisions invaded Kuwait. Over the next four months countless resolutions condemning Iraq were passed at the United Nations, culminating in Resolution 678, which overwhelmingly approved the use of all necessary means to drive Iraq from Kuwait after January 15, 1991.

King Fahd ibn Abd al-Aziz Al Saud of Saudi Arabia invited Western troops into his country on August 6, and within two days a vast buildup of aircraft and troops began, signaling the start of Operation *Desert Shield*.

Back at Tonopah, on August 17 Col Al Whitley took over command of the 37th TFW from Col Tony Tolin, and was ordered that same day to deploy the 415th to Saudi Arabia. Routing first to Langley AFB, the F-117s and their tankers were airborne again on Monday August 20 with 18 of the Black Jets, completing the nonstop haul to Saudi Arabia in 15 hours. King Khalid AB was a state-of-the-art airfield, located well beyond Iraqi Scud-B missile range, but the flying distance to Baghdad would necessitate three ARs per sortie, with a typical mission lasting five hours.

On September 5, Gen Buster Glosson presented the air campaign plan to Gen Schwarzkopf, who enthusiastically endorsed and approved it. Meanwhile, USAF aircraft acted as ferrets, flying to Iraqi border areas to stimulate their air defenses and thereby enabling communications intelligence (COMINT) and electronic intelligence (ELINT) assets to map the Iraqis' electronic air order of battle (EAOB).

The Iraqi air defense network was very sophisticated, and its destruction would chronically disable their tight central control system. Over 400 observations posts could send basic heading and altitude data to a command post. This data was supplemented by 73 radar-reporting stations feeding into 17 Intercept Operations Centers (IOCs). Four Sector Operations Centers (SOCs) then controlled the IOCs, and from these three-story, reinforced-concrete centers the defense of enormous areas of Iraq could be planned. Basic targeting information was then supplied to a vast number of missile and AAA batteries.

Following Iraq's unprovoked invasion of Kuwait, Operation *Desert Shield* saw an enormous buildup of Coalition forces positioning in theater, ready to strike should UN diplomatic efforts draw a blank. On August 19, 1990, a total of 22 F-117s flew from TTR to Langley AFB, Virginia for a one-night stopover, en route to King Khalid AB, Saudi Arabia. (Lockheed Martin)

Parked in a riveted taxiway at King Khalid AB; the base provided outstanding facilities to Senior Trend. Note the unique four-sectioned ladder provided to enable cockpit access. (USAF)

The suppression of enemy air defenses – or SEAD – was therefore the top priority in order to establish air superiority. Gen Glosson's attack plan had five objectives:

1. Destroy/disrupt C2 nodes.
2. Disrupt EW/GC1 coverage and communication.
3. Force air defense assets into autonomous modes.
4. Use expendable drones for deception.
5. Employ maximum available HARM shooters.

Like dismembering an octopus, its head – the SOCs and IOCs that ran the defense network – would be taken out by the F-117s at the outset, as would key early-warning radars and communication links. The tentacles would then be dealt with by other, non-stealthy assets. If successful, the plan would have two benefits: without the integrated defense network, SAM batteries would be forced to use their radars longer, making them more vulnerable to attack from anti-radiation missiles; and, cut off from their GCI (ground-controlled interception) controllers, Iraqi fighter pilots would become easy prey for allied air defense assets.

As the weeks ticked by, it was decided also to commit the 416th "Ghost Riders" to *Desert Shield*, and on December 4 all 20 of their aircraft arrived safely at King Khalid AB. The planners were also eager to check the effectiveness of stealth technology, so in the latter months of *Desert Shield* two F-117 pilots flew their aircraft towards the Iraqi border whilst an RC-135 Rivet Joint monitored possible Iraqi reaction. There was none until the AR tankers were instructed also to fly towards the border – the Iraqis certainly saw the tankers on their radars and immediately went into a high state of readiness. Stealth technology looked promising.

The order to "Execute Wolfpack" and implement Operation *Desert Storm* was received by the 37th Wing on the morning of January 16, 1991. "H" hour was to be 0100 Zulu (0300 hours Baghdad time). Consequently, at 0022 hours on the 17th, the first of three waves of F-117s climbed out of King Khalid AB to deliver the opening salvos of an air campaign that would not just validate the success of the F-117 and stealth technology, but would change the shape of air combat forever. Greg Feest was chosen to deliver the first bomb of *Desert Storm*, as he recalls:

My call-sign was Thunder 36 and wingman Capt. Dave "Dogman" Francis was Thunder 37. Having rendezvoused with the KC-135 tankers, we air-refuelled and headed north, towards Iraq, while flying on each wing of the tanker. At approximately 2.30am I topped off with fuel, "Stealthed-Up" my aircraft, and departed the tanker. My target was an IOC located in an underground bunker, southwest of Baghdad, near Nukhayb. This IOC was a key link between border radar sites and the air defense headquarters in Baghdad. Destroying it would allow other non-stealthy aircraft to enter Iraq undetected.

As I approached the target area, I armed my bombs and checked the aircraft's systems. I found the target on my IR display much easier than I envisioned and concentrated on tracking the target by slewing the cross hairs over the aim-point. I was able to take a glance outside the cockpit and everything was dark except for a few lights in the town. It appeared that no one knew I was in the sky. Looking back at my display, my laser began to fire as I tracked the target. I waited for the display to tell me I was "in range" and I depressed the "pickle" button. Several seconds later the weapons bay doors snapped open and I felt the 2,000lb bomb depart the aircraft. The bay door slammed closed as I watched the IR display while continuing to keep the crosshairs on the target. The bomb appeared at the bottom of the display just before it hit. At exactly 2.51am I saw the bomb go through the cross hairs and penetrate the bunker. The explosion came out of the hole the bomb had made, and blew out the doors of the bunker.

Having destroyed the target, I turned my aircraft 210 degrees left to head for my second target, an Iraqi SOC at the H-3 airfield in western Iraq. I looked out in front of my aircraft and now saw what everybody at home saw on television. Tracers, flashes, and flak were all over the place. The whole country had come alive with more triple A than I could ever imagine. I watched several SAMs launch into the sky and fly through my altitude both in front and behind me. But none of them appeared to be guided. Stealth technology really seemed to work! Even if the AAA and SAMs were not guided, the intense "barrage fire" in my target area was scary. I decided to ignore what was happening outside my jet, lowered my seat and concentrated on my displays. After all, what I couldn't see couldn't hurt me! I dropped my second bomb and turned as fast as I could back towards Saudi Arabia. I don't think I ever maneuvered the F-117A as aggressively as I did coming off my second target. For a second time in less than 30 minutes, I wanted out of the target area as fast as possible.

Despite Iraqi hardened aircraft shelters being constructed to the highest standards, they were no match for the 2,000lb GBU-27s used to such devastating effect by Senior Trend. Note how the doors of all six hangars have been blown out by the blast of the weapons exploding inside. (USAF)

Having made it safely out of the area, my thoughts turned to my wingman. Dogman was one minute behind me. I knew he had to fly through the same air defenses I had just flown through. I didn't think he would make it. For both of us to survive untouched would require too much good luck.

After hitting both targets, Feest remembers the flight back to King Khalid AB:

Just prior to crossing the border into Saudi Arabia, I performed my "destealth" procedures. My task now was to find the post-mission tanker, so I could top off with fuel and make it back to home base. After confirming the tanker was on-station and waiting for my 2-ship, I headed for the rejoin point. At a pre-designated time, I called Dogman on the radio to see if he was ready to rejoin. I prayed I would hear a response. I didn't hear an answer, so I waited several seconds and tried again. This time I heard him answer. He said he had my aircraft in sight and was ready to rejoin. Now the question was how many other Stealth Fighters would make it home. During our mission briefing, all pilots were given line up cards; these listed all the pilots flying in the first wave along with their callsigns. I had this list on my kneeboard and checked off each name as I heard the pilots check in with the tankers. After approximately 30 minutes, I looked down at the list and saw I had checked off all the names. All pilots had made it out of Iraq!

During the next 43 nights, 41 F-117s flew 1,247 sorties in 6,905 flight hours over the most highly defended targets in Iraq, achieving bombing results never before recorded – and all without the loss of, or damage to, a single aircraft.

On February 24 at 0300 hours (local time), the Coalition ground assault began. In true blitzkrieg fashion, it was all over in just three days. On February 27 Kuwait City was liberated and a ceasefire declared. At the end of the Gulf War, Gen Buster Glosson noted: "Reflecting on the Gulf War, and specifically the F-117 and what it was able to accomplish; only one word seems appropriate: awesome."

Leading the first element of eight F-117As to return home from King Khalid AB, Col Al Whitley and two KC-10s, containing 130 support personnel, touched down at Nellis AFB in front of a crowd of 25,000 on April 1, 1991. During the following months, all but a handful of the 37th's F-117As returned home – those remaining in Saudi Arabia making up the backbone of Operation *Southern Watch*. To man the F-117A deployment, a three-month rotation cycle was established for some 200 pilots, maintenance staff, and other key personnel.

The move to Holloman

Having demonstrated its incredible capabilities to the world during *Desert Storm*, the F-117 took another tentative step into the White World

E **FIRST BOMB OF *DESERT STORM***
On the night of January 16/17, 1991, "Thunder 36," flown by Lt Col Greg Feest releases the first bomb at the beginning of Operation *Desert Storm*. The 2,000lb laser guided GBU-27 exploded on target – an Intercept Operations Centre (IOC), in an underground bunker located southwest of Baghdad, near Nukhayb. The aircraft was completely undetected, but after the weapon exploded "all hell let loose" in the form of non-radar-directed 23mm, 37mm and 57mm AAA fire through which Feest had no option but to fly.

Aircraft 826 first flew on March 2, 1987. During Operation *Desert Storm* the aircraft ratcheted up 29 operational missions and was named Nachtfalke. It is seen here touching down at Holloman AFB whilst allocated to the 9th FS, "The Flying Knights." (USAF)

when, in order to reduce high operating costs incurred from utilizing such a remote site, it was decided to relocate from Tonopah to Holloman AFB, New Mexico. Consequently, on July 8, 1992, the 37th FW at TTR participated in both the base's inactivation ceremony and its commensurate deactivation, with its assets transferring across to the 49th FW. Command of the wing was also transferred from Al Whitley to Brig-Gen Lloyd "Fig" Newton. The move to Holloman reunited families, enabling them to join their loved ones in living quarters on or close to the base. It also eradicated the need for Key Airlines to shuttle over 2,500 personnel on 75 weekly flights to and from their place of work – an action that would in itself save millions of dollars a year.

On August 4, 1992, the first Holloman-based F-117A was lost in an accident. Capt John B. Mills of the 416th FS was forced to eject from aircraft 801, after it entered an uncommanded roll and caught fire. The crash occurred just eight miles (12km) northwest of Holloman, and Mills landed safely just half a mile from the blazing wreckage. A crash investigation identified the cause as an improperly reinstalled bleed air duct, which led to a hydraulic line malfunction to the flight controls and a fire.

The move to Holloman also signaled a steady integration of the F-117A into theater operational planning, enabling it to become a true "force multiplier," something that was impossible to achieve during its years in the "black." Accordingly, from March 15 to 26, 1993, four F-117s from the 416th FS participated in Exercise *Team Spirit*, a short deployment to Kunsan AB, South Korea. Three months later, between June 13 and 17, eight of the black jets from the 415th FS participated in *Coronet Havoc* and deployed to Gilze-Rijen in the Netherlands. (F-117s participated in their first Red Flag exercise – 94-2 – between February 8 and 17, 1994.)

On July 30, 1993, the F-117 units underwent another redesignation when the 415th and 416th Fighter squadrons became the 9th and 8th Fighter squadrons, respectively. This was followed in December 1993 by a redesignation of the training unit, the 417th, which became the 7th FS.

The 49th lost its second F-117A from Holloman (the fifth to date) on May 10, 1995, at 2225 hours. Aircraft 822 was being flown by Capt Ken Levens of the 9th FS on a night training flight when contact was lost. The aircraft crashed on Red Mesa, at the Zuri Indian Reservation. Yet again the pilot had not attempted to eject prior to the crash, and an accident investigation team established that there were no signs of mechanical or electrical failure prior to impact. Pilot disorientation seemed, yet again, to be the most likely cause of the tragedy.

The Balkans

The collapse of European communism and the subsequent breakup of Yugoslavia triggered a series of bloody wars in the region as ethnic groups within the fledgling states of Slovenia, Croatia, and Bosnia-Herzegovina sought independence from Belgrade and from each other. Serbian President Milosevic stirred up nationalism to incite the large Serbian populations in Bosnia-Herzegovina and Croatia to unite in a bid to create a "Greater Serbia." Eventually a UN Protection Force (UNPROFOR) was sent to provide humanitarian assistance in "safe areas." Despite several UN resolutions, the Serbs continued to gain ground, and many atrocities were committed in the process.

During this same period, member states of NATO agreed to a new, post-Cold War remit resulting in the formation of a "New Strategic Concept." This enabled NATO to go beyond collective defense to conduct new security missions, including peacekeeping and conflict prevention. As the Bosnian War continued to escalate in brutality, Operation *Deliberate Force* was launched by NATO in the early morning of August 30, 1995, with a series of precision air strikes against selected targets in Serb-held areas. The air campaign ended on September 20, after Bosnian-Serb forces sued for peace. This led to the Dayton Accord, which was signed in Paris on December 14, 1995.

Unfortunately the Dayton Accord did not signal an end to hostilities in the Balkans, which again erupted in Kosovo in late 1998. On January 30, 1999, NATO stated that it would take whatever steps were necessary, including air strikes, to compel Serbian compliance with UN Security Resolution 1199 (passed on September 23, 1998), aimed at achieving a peaceful political solution in Kosovo. As NATO air forces continued their buildup, the 8th FS deployed 12 F-117s from Holloman to Aviano AB, Italy on February 20. Peace talks failed, and the Serb offensive in Kosovo intensified. The NATO Supreme Allied Commander Europe (SACEUR), US Army Gen Wesley Clark, was ordered to initiate air strikes in the Federal Republic of Yugoslavia, signaling the beginning of Operation *Allied Force*.

On March 24, 1999, allied air strikes began. The tactics implemented, however, differed significantly from those used so decisively in *Desert Storm*. To begin with, electronic countermeasure (ECM) coverage was significantly reduced following early retirement of the USAF EF-111 Ravens. Lt-Gen Michael Short USAF (overall air commander) was extremely restricted when it came to target selection due to political interference. He was also forbidden to route strike packages over Bosnia, forcing them instead to ingress and egress through just two narrow corridors. Finally, President Clinton and

On February 21, 1999, 12 F-117s from the 8th FS arrived at Aviano AB, Italy to support Operation *Allied Force*, as part of the 31st Air Expeditionary Wing. (USAF, Senior Airman Mitch Fuqua)

On the night of April 17/18, 1999, during Operation *Allied Force*, Lt-Col William "Brad" O'Connor of the 8th FS flew aircraft 788 and attacked two targets. The first attack depicted here was against the Baric munitions plant, situated a few miles west of Belgrade, on the banks of the Sava River; his second attack was against a large gas sphere on the edge of the Novi Sad oil refinery. Equipped with two 2,000lb GBU-10s, O'Connor's callsign for this mission was Vega 02. The desired munitions point of impact (DMPI) for the first target was a mixing tower surrounded on all four sides by a large earth berm. Taken from the aircraft's infrared targeting system, the first frame shows the small white rectangle at the center of the crosshairs centered on the tower. With less than five seconds to impact, the laser has automatically transitioned to the auto-fire mode and illuminated the target for the weapon's Paveway-2 seeker head. The bomb (the black streak just off the six o'clock position) has cleared the "protective" earth berm and will impact the target about 30 degrees off the vertical. The second frame records a direct hit with the weapon in full detonation and the attack display flooded with energy, obscuring the view of the target – a phenomena known as "blooming." The second attack also resulted in a direct hit. (Lt-Col Brad O'Connor)

other western European leaders mistakenly believed that a limited, collective show of force would be enough to convince Milosevic to sue for peace. Consequently, air strikes got off to a sluggish start, and these highly "corseted" operating procedures, coupled with Serb ingenuity, were to have dire consequences for Senior Trend.

Vega 31

Much of the following information has been made available to the author by Gabor Zord, a Hungarian journalist, who has spent several years researching this conflict and has been able to dispel much of the misinformation surrounding this particular incident.

Lt-Col Zoltan Dani was commander of the 3rd Battalion, 250th Serbian Air Defense Missile Brigade, equipped with S-125 Neva-M (SA-3 GOA) surface-to-air missiles. The mobile system consisted of a P-18 "Spoon Rest-D" early warning radar, capable of utilizing pre-programmed, pre-authorized frequencies in the VHF A-band range of around 150 MHz. This radar was used to locate a target initially in azimuth and range only. Once acquired, the target would then be handed over to the operators of the Low Bow missile guidance radar system of the SA-3, utilizing the I-band frequency range. Low Bow would then begin its own target acquisition, resolving azimuth, range, elevation, and velocity based upon details supplied by Spoon Rest. Once acquired, Low Bow would be set to tracking mode, and at this point the system was ready to launch a missile. Once fired, the missiles in this case operated in a three-point guidance mode, utilizing guidance commands transmitted to the missile via a radio data link.

Aware of the looming conflict with NATO, Lt-Col Dani knew his unit would be targeted by allied F-16s and Tornadoes tasked with SEAD. He therefore trained his unit rigorously to achieve a 90-minute total equipment breakdown, in readiness to move to another location – mobility would be the key to survival. For additional insurance against HARM (High-Speed Anti-Radiation Missile) attacks, he insisted that his unit restrict operation of their high-frequency Low Blow radar to a maximum 20-second burst before shutting down. Understanding the relationship between the size of a radar's wavelength verses the dimensions of the target, Dani had tried to convince higher headquarters to allow him to alter circuits in the P-18. This would have enabled it to access even lower frequencies, thereby increasing the resonance of a low observable F-117 return, but his requests were ignored.

On the afternoon of March 24, Lt-Col Dani received orders to move his

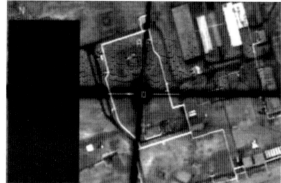

battalion from their peacetime location at Jakovo and deploy to a reserve area near Simanovci, west of Belgrade. There the unit lay low to await further instructions. (Jakovo was destroyed by an F-117 or B-2 first strike raid that same night – over 90 missiles in storage at the site exploded.) Then, on the afternoon of March 27, the 250th received orders to go to alert and were given instructions as to which four VHF A-band frequencies they were to use.

Meanwhile, Lt-Col Dale Zelko of the 8th FS got airborne from Aviano in F-117 serial number 82-0806, callsign Vega 31. Part of an eight-ship first-strike package bound for the northern part of the country, he was to hit a well-defended air defense node in the southern suburbs of Belgrade. The weather that night was "challenging," forcing the cancellation of other support/strike aircraft which critically included HARM-toting F-16s and Tornadoes. It is also understood that EA-6 Prowlers, scheduled to provide an ECM cloak, were repositioned in readiness to cover a later B-2 strike.

Seated in front of VIKO, his remote radar display of the P-18, Lt-Col Dani received notification from the 250th Brigade's combat center that "Aircraft are in the air." Dani ordered the P-18 to be activated and instructed the operators to use the lowest allocated VHF frequency. The battery acquired four targets at a distance of between 25 and 30km almost immediately, and it was clear from the return characteristics that they had located an LO aircraft. Soon one of these targets entered the engagement zone of the missile system, and Dani ordered its acquisition with the Low Blow radar. Manual tracking operators caught a glimpse of the return, before losing it. They reacquired it, only to lose it once again, before finally gaining a steady lock on the target. During these acquisition attempts, Dani decided to transgress his self-imposed 20-second shutdown rule and stay on air, since there were no non-stealthy returns in the area – thereby ruling out the possibility of a HARM attack. At 1940 Zulu (GMT), 2040 hours local time, Vega 31 had its bomb bay doors open (creating a large corner reflector), and was on target run-in. An all-stations warning transmission from AWACS advising "Firefly-three, Firefly-three" (activation of an SA-3 site) in Lt-Col Zelko's vicinity was made; the F-117 fleet was not equipped with radar warning and homing (RWAH) equipment. However, just seconds away from release, the pilot was concentrating solely on tracking the target through the DLIR sight. Once the GBU-27 had hit the target, and with 806's bomb bay doors closed, the aircraft went into a hard, preplanned left turn.

In its hard turn, the F-117's angular speed dramatically increased from Dani's perspective, adding further complexity to the intercept solution. With the Low Blow tracking radar engaged, Dani gave the order to fire a salvo of two V-601P type missiles in a three-to-five second interval. In the cockpit, Zelko recalls visually tracking two missiles as they blasted through the thin vale of cloud beneath and instinctively thought, "This is bad." The lead missile (actually the second SA-3 to be fired, which failed to lock on to Low Blow's data link and went into a ballistic trajectory) passed over the

This is the actual facility, commanded by Lt-Col Zoltan Dani, that successfully engaged and shot down Vega 31. (Gabor Zord)

The wreckage of 82-0806, the only F-117 lost in combat. The aircraft hit the ground inverted and at an almost flat angle. (Via *Air Forces Monthly*)

aircraft, so close that Zelko could feel its shockwave buffeting the F-117. Zelko quickly reacquired the second missile (the first to have been fired, which was guiding) and in doing so realized that it was going to run right into him. The impact and effect was extremely violent, blowing most of the left wing off the F-117 and slamming it into a left roll and a 7 negative-g tuck. The negative-g forces were such that Zelko found it almost impossible to get his hands down to the side ejection handles, and to this day does not recall the 18g kick that sent his ejection seat up the rails.

Just 1.8 seconds later, Zelko was hanging beneath a fully deployed chute. Believing his early capture to be inevitable, he decided to use his basic survival radio (equipped with neither secure-voice nor an over-the-horizon capability) whilst still on the descent to relay his estimated position on the guard frequency (UHF 234.0 MHz). This would ensure that allied forces knew he had managed to eject safely, and would energize search and rescue (SAR) assets.

Landing in a field near the village of Budjanovci, 200–300 yards (180–270m) away from a busy road, Zelko's luck held. After some four hours on the ground, he was plucked from under the Serbs' noses by a USAF rescue team consisting of two MH-53s and one MH-60.

On April 3, 1999, thirteen F-117s from the 9th FS joined Operation *Allied Force* when they deployed from Holloman to Spangdahlem AB, Germany. It has come to light that an aircraft from this unit (possibly aircraft 82-0818) was damaged in the left wing by either a Serb SAM or AAA, during an attack sometime between April 4 and 9. The damage was such that it is believed the pilot was required to divert. This incident remains a highly sensitive issue and both Lockheed and USAF personnel have refused point-blank to elaborate further.

F

THE YUGOSLAV LOSS

On March 27, 1999, whilst participating in Operation *Allied Force*, F-117 serial 82-0806, flown by Lt-Col Dale Zelko, was shot down by a Serbian SA-3. Zelko had just dropped his ordnance and was in a pre-programmed left blanked turn when the missile struck. The force of the explosion blew away most of the aircraft's left wing and slammed the F-117 into a left roll and a 7 negative-g tuck. Despite this, Zelko was able to eject successfully from the aircraft and was later rescued by USAF Special Forces. This would prove to be the only F-117 lost in combat.

Operation *Allied Force* was brought to a successful conclusion, and hostilities ended on June 10, 1999. During the 80 days of combat, F-117s completed 760 operational sorties. Yugoslav forces agreed to withdraw from Kosovo and make way for an international peace presence.

Operations *Iraqi Freedom* and *Enduring Freedom*

Following the end of Operation *Desert Storm* in February 1991, the USAF maintained a continuous presence in the region, enforcing two no-fly zones over Iraq: one to the north based out of Turkey, termed Operation *Northern Watch*, and the other to the south, policed from bases in Kuwait and Saudi Arabia, named Operation *Southern Watch*.

Following Iraqi threats to shoot down U-2 reconnaissance aircraft undertaking missions on behalf of the UN, F-117s became involved in *Southern Watch* under an operation named *Desert Thunder*. This consisted of two specific deployments under Operation *Desert Strike*. Based at Ahmed al-Jaber, a forward operating location in Kuwait just 45 miles (70km) from the Iraq border, the first deployment involved six F-117s from the 8th FS from November 19, 1997, to March 1998. The second deployment by the 9th FS involved another six of the "Black Jets" running from February 13 to June 8, 1998. The direct flight from Holloman lasted 16.5 hours, establishing yet another Senior Trend milestone – the longest nonstop flight to date. The deployment was extremely successful, as Saddam Hussein's forces backed down and did not proceed with the shoot-down threat.

Following terrorist attacks in the United States on September 11, 2001, and the overthrow of the Taliban and al-Qaeda in Afghanistan, the US turned its attention once more to Iraq and the regime of Saddam Hussein. Citing intelligence information that would later prove highly controversial, it was claimed that Iraq had stockpiles of weapons of mass destruction (WMD). In 2002 the UN Security Council passed Resolution 1441, and after weeks of playing cat and mouse with the UN inspection team, allied patience with the Iraqi dictator ran out. The stated political goal of Operation *Iraqi Freedom* was the removal of Saddam Hussein's regime and the destruction of its ability to use, or make available, WMD.

On the evening of March 19, an intelligence report was received at short notice, stating that Saddam Hussein and other top regime leaders would be staying overnight at the Dora Farms bunker complex southwest of Baghdad. The J-2 intelligence cell within the Combined Air Operations Center (CAOC) at Prince Sultan AB, Saudi Arabia, provided target information, including GPS coordinates. It then directed that two F-117s of the 8th Expeditionary Fighter Squadron, 379th Air Expeditionary Wing, based at Al Udeid AB, Qatar, should be made ready for the strike, and that each aircraft should be equipped with two enhanced guided-bomb units (EGBU-27 "bunker-busters"). These 2,000lb "enhanced" weapons featured a GPS/INS guidance system, enabling them to be dropped accurately through

The spoils of war: Lt-Col Dani sits atop some of the wreckage recovered from Lt-Col Zelko's F-117 and Lt-Col Goldfein's F-16C – both aircraft having fallen victim to his SA-3 battery. (Lt-Col Zoltan Dani)

cloud cover, without the pilot having to visually acquire and lase the target. The weapons, however, were very new to the F-117 and had never been tested before in combat – indeed they had only arrived at Al Udeid a mere 24 hours earlier.

Just two hours after receiving the intelligence report an execution order arrived, and two F-117s, flown by the 8th FS commander Lt-Col Dave Toomey and Maj Mark Hoehn (callsigns Ram 01 and Ram 02), were airborne at 0338 hours (local time). Whilst over the Gulf, near Kuwait City, they rendezvoused with a KC-135 and topped up their tanks. They were also joined by three USN EA-6B Prowlers to provide ECM support and two HARM-equipped F-16s. Clearing the tanker, Ram 01 and 02 split up, taking different routes to their common target. Thirteen minutes after dawn had broken over Baghdad, at 0530 hours, each of the F-117s released two EGBU-27s through early morning cloud, completely catching the Iraqi air defenses off guard. Post-strike reconnaissance revealed that the four bombs slammed into the bunker, situated underneath a field, just 50ft (15m) apart in a square pattern, leaving much of the earth on top undisturbed. The bombs had worked as advertised, and the two pilots each received a DFC for an outstanding mission executed with minimal lead times. The mission's intended target, however, was not in residence.

On April 6, 2003, just 18 days after the beginning of Operation *Iraqi Freedom*, the Coalition leadership were able to declare complete air supremacy over Iraq. Ten days later, the first humanitarian relief flight landed at Bashur AB. This action would prove to be the F-117's final combat operation. In total 82 sorties were flown by F-117s. The EGBU-27 became the weapon of choice, and 98 were dropped. Although it was undoubtedly a highly successful swansong, the platform was not utilized in the campaign to the same level as in previous operations – perhaps reflecting the number of other stand-off weapon systems options that were now available to the military planners.

THE PROGRAM SHUTDOWN

The legendary achievements of Lockheed's F-117 will ensure that the aircraft's place in military aeronautical history is secure. However, the relentless development and application of more complex computer modeling and other technologies have now surpassed those used in the facet-based stealth technology of the 1970s. Additionally, the changing political climate, with

Following a flying career spanning nearly 24 years, aircraft 782 was retired by the USAF in October 2005. Prior to being delivered to Holloman AFB as a maintenance trainer, members of the 410th Flight Test Squadron repainted the aircraft in the stars and bars, as worn by the same aircraft back in December 1983. (USAF/Steve Zapka)

Although retired from active service, the F-117 fleet is kept in storage inside some of the hangars back at their former home at TTR. (Via James Goodall)

inherent, ongoing defense spending cuts, inevitably ensnared the F-117.

The USAF originally planned to retire the F-117 in 2011, but the platform was maintenance-intensive. In Program Budget Decision (PBD) 720, dated December 28, 2005, it was proposed that retirement of the entire fleet should be brought forward to October 2008 to facilitate the purchase of additional F-22 Raptors. PBD 720 envisaged a two-phase F-117 drawdown, with ten aircraft being retired in fiscal year (FY) 2007 and the remaining 42 in FY 2008; it stated that there were now more capable LO assets in the inventory and that these possessed an enhanced precision penetrating weapons capability – they included the B-2, F-22, and JASSM. Implementation of the plan would, it was estimated, save $1.07 billion and the decommissioning process would occur in eight phases, with the first operational aircraft phase beginning on March 13, 2007, and the final wave leaving on April 22, 2008. Consequently, as part of PBD 720, on December 31, 2006, the F-117's Formal Training Unit (FTU), the 7th FS, was officially deactivated and the first of ten Nighthawks were grounded whilst their bed-down base was being prepared. Unlike most other US military aircraft, the F-117s would not be going to the 309th Aerospace Maintenance and Regeneration Group (AMARG) at Davis-Monthan AFB, Arizona; instead, due to many aspects of the aircraft still remaining classified, they would be retired to their original home at TTR. The 8th FS was deactivated on April 22, 2008, followed finally by the 9th on May 16 that year.

Four F-117s remained with the 410th FLTS at Palmdale for flight-test purposes, but by the beginning of August just two remained. The last F-117 to leave Palmdale was aircraft 86-0831, which duly arrived at Tonopah on August 11, 2008 – the 410th having been deactivated in a ceremony on August 1.

On arrival at TTR, the aircraft had their wings removed and they were placed at the back of their original, climate-controlled hangars. This level of care clearly paid off, as four F-117s have subsequently been reactivated, and at the time of writing are participating in a test project involving Lockheed Martin at Area 51. Not surprisingly, no other details have yet been made available.

CONCLUSION

Even though the raw science behind reducing an aircraft's radar signature was available to both major power blocs during the Cold War, it was the United States that decided to fully understand, embrace, develop, and exploit the military potential behind these new technologies. The result was one of just a handful of truly transformational developments that have occurred in the history of military aviation – the world's first truly stealthy combat aircraft. The reduced radar signature of Lockheed's F-117 produced an exploitable advantage way beyond that of any contemporary strike aircraft.

The security surrounding Have Blue and Senior Trend was spectacularly successful in keeping what was recognized as a "perishable resource" totally under wraps from 1975 until it was decided to release basic information about the F-117 in November 1988. Parallel developments in fly-by-wire technology and the all-important IRADS, including the FLIR and DLIR turrets, were also crucial to the aircraft's success as a viable weapons system.

The culmination of this effort to facilitate the F-117's great success on the battlefield, combined with the professionalism and dedication of all those involved in the two programs, was made apparent on the night of January 17, 1991, when the first "Black Jets" released their laser-guided ordnance on targets in Iraq, at the beginning of Operation *Desert Storm*. By the end of that air campaign, F-117s had flown in excess of 1,200 combat missions without loss or damage to a single aircraft – testament indeed to this outstanding milestone in military aviation.

History teaches us that military advantages are finite. Flying during Operation *Allied Force*, under conditions of tight route restriction and without the comprehensive level of ECM and HARM support enjoyed during *Desert Storm*, and with the enemy's greater understanding of stealth and his practical ingenuity, the F-117 became vulnerable. The Serbs successfully engaged and destroyed one of the "Black Jets" and damaged another, effectively demonstrating what Lockheed had always maintained – that the F-117 fielded LO technology and was *not invisible* to radar.

Without doubt the Lockheed F-117 achieved a level of combat success seldom seen before or since. Its development and deployment put the rest of the world on the back foot, forcing all future combat aircraft design teams to consider the incorporation of at least some element of this groundbreaking platform's capability.

The strides that have taken place in software development since the mid-1970s have enabled aircraft designers to further build upon the technologies first validated by Senior Trend. A number of current technology demonstrators point to a near-to-mid future of stealthy, network-centric, high-performance unmanned combat air vehicles (UCAVs) able to strike accurately at targets in non-permissive airspace, using non-boresight, GPS-guided munitions from stand-off ranges. Lockheed Martin's research into an affordable, stealthy, unmanned, hypersonic intelligence, surveillance, and reconnaissance (ISR) platform (the so-called SR-72) has the makings of another success story, and many of these advances can be directly attributed to the remarkable Lockheed F-117.

BIBLIOGRAPHY

Crickmore, Paul F. and Alison J., *F-117 Nighthawk*, MBI (1999)

Gordon, Michael R. and Trainor, General Bernard E., *The Generals' War: The Inside Story of the Conflict in the Gulf*, Back Bay Books (1995)

Henneman, MSgt Greg, *Nighthawk Compendium: A Reference History of the F-117 Program*, US Air Force (2006)

Mailes, Yancy D. and Landis, Tony R., *F-117 Nighthawk Stealth Fighter Photo Scrapbook*, Specialty Press (2006)

O'Connor, Lt-Col William B., *Stealth Fighter: A Year in the Life of an F-117 Pilot*, Zenith Press (2012)

Thompson, Warren E., *Bandits over Baghdad*, Speciality Press (2000)

USAF F-117 Aircraft Utility Flight Manual, USAF (1992)

INDEX

Figures in **bold** refer to illustrations.